Napoleon's Infantry

Napoleon's Infantry

French Line, Light and
Foreign Regiments 1799–1815

Gabriele Esposito

Pen & Sword
MILITARY

First published in Great Britain in 2022
by Pen & Sword Military
An imprint of Pen & Sword Books Limited
47 Church Street
Barnsley
South Yorkshire
S70 2AS

ISBN 978 1 39900 831 0

A CIP catalogue record for this book is
available from the British Library

Typeset in Adobe Caslon
by Mac Style

Printed and bound in India by Replika Press Pvt. Ltd.

Pen & Sword Books Limited incorporates the imprints of Atlas,
Archaeology, Aviation, Discovery, Family History, Fiction, History, Maritime,
Military, Military Classics, Politics, Select, Transport, True Crime, Air World,
Frontline Publishing, Leo Cooper, Remember When, Seaforth Publishing,
The Praetorian Press, Wharncliffe Local History, Wharncliffe Transport,
Wharncliffe True Crime and White Owl.

For a complete list of Pen & Sword titles please contact
PEN & SWORD BOOKS LIMITED
47 Church Street, Barnsley, South Yorkshire, S70 2AS, England
E-mail: enquiries@pen-and-sword.co.uk
Website: www. pen-and-sword.co.uk

Contents

Gabriele Esposito is a military historian who works as a freelance author and researcher for some of the most important publishing houses in the military history sector. In particular, he is an expert specializing in uniformology: his interests and expertise range from the ancient civilizations to modern post-colonial conflicts. During recent years, he has conducted and published several researches on the military history of the Latin American countries, with special attention on the War of the Triple Alliance and the War of the Pacific. He is among the leading experts on the military history of the Italian Wars of Unification and the Spanish Carlist Wars. His books and essays are published on a regular basis by Osprey Publishing, Winged Hussar Publishing and Libreria Editrice Goriziana; he is also the author of numerous military history articles appearing in specialized magazines like *Ancient Warfare Magazine*, *Medieval Warfare Magazine*, *The Armourer*, *History of War*, *Guerres et Histoire*, *Focus Storia* and *Focus Storia Wars*.

Acknowledgements

This book is dedicated to my parents, Maria Rosaria and Benedetto, for the immense love and great support that they have given me during all the days of my life. A very special thanks goes to Philip Sidnell, the commissioning editor of my books for Pen & Sword: his love for military history and his passion for publishing are fundamental for the success of our publications. A special mention goes to the production manager of this title, Matt Jones, for his hard work and great competence. Many thanks also to copy-editor Tony Walton, for his precious help and for his friendship. All the pictures published in this book are public domain ones obtained from the magnificent Digital Collections of the New York Public Library. Everyone with an interest in military history can easily browse the vast contents of the latter at https://digitalcollections.nypl.org/.

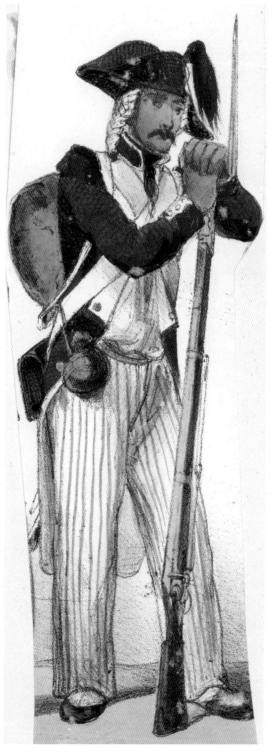 

Grenadier of the line infantry with 1793 dress.

Fusilier of the line infantry with 1793 uniform.

Grenadier of the line
infantry with 1793 dress.

Introduction

The main aim of this book is to present a detailed overview of the history, organization and uniforms of the French infantry during the Napoleonic Period. Our analysis will start with a description of the French foot troops' evolution during the years 1789–99, but will later focus on the years that saw the ascendancy and the fall of Napoleon's military power (1799–1815). The infantrymen of the Emperor Napoleon were not all elite soldiers like the members of his Imperial Guard, they did not wear the dashing uniforms of his cavalry and they were not beloved by Napoleon like his artillerymen. However, it was the infantry of the French Army that effectively won most of the battles during the glorious years from 1799–1812. The French common infantryman was intelligent, aggressive, well-disciplined and extremely resilient: he had total trust in his overall commander and was determined to export the ideals of the Revolution to the other countries of Europe with the point of his bayonet. During the eighteenth century, infantry had played a crucial role on European battlefields, in mighty clashes that were a perfect example of the so-called 'lace wars', with thousands of disciplined soldiers – all professionals, and many of them mercenaries – marching in perfect order and firing upon the enemy formations with great regularity; this was the tactic of the foot troops during the century of the Enlightenment. During this time, the leading European royal families struggled against each other for domination of the continent and had their own dynastic armies, which were more like private military forces than national armies in the modern sense of the word. The life of civilians was generally not affected by the ongoing wars, which were seen as private affairs between monarchs. Members of the aristocracy provided the commanding officers of the various military units, but spent very little of their time learning how to train and lead their men. The NCOs and rankers were mostly professionals, who earned a living by fighting for money rather than for a cause. War had its basic rules, which were common to all the European nobles: the idea of 'total war' did not yet exist, and on several occasions military campaigns were simply an instrument of diplomacy.

This situation came to an end in 1792, when the French Revolution started to decisively transform the existing military systems. In 1789, much of the French population rose up in revolt against Louis XVI, one of Europe's absolute monarchs.

Fusiliers of the line infantry in 1805; the figure on the right has a winter greatcoat.

Uniforms of the line infantry in 1805 (from left to right): voltigeur, officer, grenadier and fusilier.

New political ideas were spreading enthusiasm among the people, and the new social class of the bourgeoisie was emerging as the leading force of French society. There was no longer space for the privileges of the aristocracy and the rich clergy: a new middle-class, well educated and much advanced, wanted to become the protagonist of France's political life. Some years before these events in France, the settlers of the Thirteen Colonies in North America had shown that it was possible to change the existing social order by fighting for freedom: now, in France, every subject wanted to be a citizen and wanted to enjoy certain new rights. The royal government could no longer exert absolute power: the rights of each free man were sanctioned in a constitution (something that the people of England had enjoyed for several centuries) and the participation of the citizens in the political life of their country was made through a representative body – the national assembly or parliament. By 1792, after three years of revolution, the French population had already achieved their main objectives, but now the new French state came under attack from other European countries. These nations feared that the French Revolution could penetrate across their borders, dethroning other royal families around Europe. During 1792, the new army of Revolutionary France faced a coalition force led by Prussia at the Battle of Valmy, where, against all odds, the well-drilled professional soldiers of the 'lace wars', who had been forged by Frederick the Great, were humiliated by the new troops of the French bourgeoisie. From that moment on, the humble but splendid French infantrymen won one victory after the other, after 1796 often under the guidance of the genial and ambitious Napoleon. An entire army had completely changed its nature in just a few years and would dominate the battlefields of Europe for two decades. But how was this possible? And how did the French infantryman become so effective and so superior to his opponent? To find an answer to these questions, a wide range of factors have to be taken into account, starting from the early days of the French Revolution. For what Napoleon inherited when he became First Consul in 1799 was a French Army that had already been completely reformed.

Chapter 1

The French Infantry from 1789–92

During the eighteenth century, France was one of Europe's leading military powers. From the time of Louis XIV – the 'Sun King' – the French monarch had always deployed large military forces on the battlefields of Europe, playing a pivotal role in the politics of the continent. With the ascendancy of Frederick the Great and of Prussia, however, the excellent reputation of the French Army had gradually started to decline. During the Seven Years' War of 1756–63, in fact, French troops were defeated on several occasions by the Prussians in Europe and by the British in North America. These defeats were not caused by a single factor, but by a series of elements, primarily because the basic French soldier was inferior to his Prussian or British equivalent in terms of training and morale. The organization and weaponry of the French Army were still excellent, but something had changed in the relationship between the troops and the ruling royal family, with the wars fought by France being perceived as dynastic struggles by most of the French population, which had negative consequences for the morale of the soldiers. Monarchs such as Louis XV fought wars more for their personal glory than for the good of France as a nation. Consequently, most of the rank-and-file troops were seeking new motivations and of new ideals. During the final years of the American Revolution, France sent a major expeditionary corps to the rebelling Thirteen Colonies in order to support George Washington's Continental Army that was fighting the British. Fascinated by the ideals of their American comrades and led by some intelligent officers, the French soldiers in North America fought extremely well and played a crucial role in the decisive defeat of the British at Yorktown in 1781. When they returned home, they brought with them not only the laurels of victory but a series of new ideas about freedom and democracy. Although the American expedition was a military success for France, it had disastrous consequences economically, as by the end of it the kingdom was on the verge of bankruptcy and in need of a series of urgent reforms. The conflict against Britain in North America was therefore one of the main causes behind the outbreak of the French Revolution, as well as a turning point in the history of the French Army. It became clear that the potential of the French soldiers was still great, but that the Army needed new ideals in order to regain its previous prominence on the battlefields of Europe.

Uniforms of the fusiliers (from left to right): fusilier in 1805, fusilier with greatcoat in 1805, fusilier with 1806 shako, fusilier with greatcoat and 1810 shako, and fusilier with 1812 dress.

The infantry was the most important and most numerous component of the French Army by the end of the eighteenth century, as in all other major European armies. By 1789, it comprised 102 regiments, of which twenty-three were made up of foreign mercenaries: eleven Swiss, eight German, three Irish and one Belgian. Since the days of Louis XIV, the French Army had always comprised a sizeable number of foreign units, which were made up of professional soldiers who sold their services to the French royal family. The Swiss, who had been hired as mercenaries by the French since the closing years of the fifteenth century, were an organic component of

Drummer (left)
and officer
(right) of the
line infantry
with winter
greatcoat.

the French Army by 1789. They were well trained and well disciplined, as were the German mercenaries, who came from the various princedoms of the Holy Roman Empire. The Irish regiments were the last heirs of the 'Irish Army in exile' that was organized in France by the Jacobites following the ascendancy of William of Orange to the throne of England, Scotland and Ireland in 1689. After the occupation of Ireland by King William following the Glorious Revolution, a number of Irishmen abandoned their homeland over the succeeding years in order to enlist in the French Army. France was the mortal enemy of Britain, and the French monarchs supported all the Jacobite uprisings that took place in the British Isles during the eighteenth century. The presence of Irish soldiers in the French Army was thus mostly due to political reasons. The single Belgian regiment came from the city of Liége, the only major urban centre of Belgium that was not part of the Holy Roman Empire, retaining its status as an independent ecclesiastical princedom. Meanwhile, there were seventy-nine infantry regiments in the French Army made up of soldiers from France, an impressive number by contemporary European standards. Most of the infantry units were stationed on the borders of the kingdom or around Paris, but 10,000 of them were dispersed among the French colonies that were located across the world.

According to the new internal organization that was introduced between 1786 and 1788, each infantry regiment of the French Army consisted of a regimental staff plus two battalions. Only one regiment, the 'Régiment du Roi' or 'King's Regiment', was an exception to this rule, having a larger establishment with four battalions. A single battalion comprised one elite company and four line companies. The 1st Battalion of a regiment had a company of grenadiers (heavy infantry) as its elite company, while the 2nd Battalion had an elite company of chasseurs (light infantry). The single company of chasseurs of each regiment comprised six carabiniers, or sharpshooters, who were the only soldiers of the unit to be armed with rifled carbines and not with smoothbore muskets. In peacetime, the standard establishment of an infantry regiment was 1,202 men, which was increased to 2,642 in the event of mobilization for war, with the number of soldiers in each company being doubled and a new depot company being organized in case of conflict. In addition to the line infantry, there were the infantry regiments of the Royal Guard (the French Guards and the Swiss Guards), as well as the auxiliary corps of the Provincial Troops and the Militia. The Troupes Provinciales consisted of second-line units that were recruited and garrisoned in the various provinces of the Kingdom of France: they made up a reserve of 75,000 well-trained semi-professional soldiers who could be called to serve in case of war in order to perform auxiliary duties. The infantry of the Provincial Troops comprised thirteen regiments of grenadiers, fourteen regiments of fusiliers and seventy-nine garrison battalions, the latter mainly garrisoning the royal fortifications and military bases that were scattered around French territory. The Milice, or Militia, were recruited in the countryside from unmarried male peasants between the ages of 18 and 40, who were selected by lottery. They were assembled for just a few days every year and consisted of third-line units that existed only on paper. While the soldiers of the regular infantry were all volunteers or mercenaries, those of the Militia were recruited according to an embryonic form of conscription, which was particularly unpopular even though members of the Milice were only called to serve for a handful of days annually. The Provincial Troops, meanwhile, were placed somewhere between the regulars and the militiamen. They had been organized for the first time in 1771 and were completely restructured in 1778 in order to act as a strategic reserve for the regulars. Their members were recruited like those of the Militia, but mostly came from urban centres rather than the countryside, and they also underwent more substantial training and thus could be considered as semi-professional soldiers. Each of the seventy-nine garrison battalions of the Provincial Troops was attached to one regiment of regular infantry and acted as the latter's depot.

During the eighteenth century, especially in the turbulent years of the Seven Years' War, a new kind of infantry started to appear on European battlefields: the light infantry. This consisted of soldiers who had a higher degree of mobility compared to the line infantrymen and were trained to fight in open order as opposed to in line or in column like the standard fusiliers. The main tactical function of the light infantrymen was to act as skirmishers on the battlefield, so they were usually deployed in front or on the flanks of the line infantry formations. During the Seven Year's War, the light corps of the Austrian Army, recruited from the Balkan territories of the Habsburgs, had shown their potential against the excellent Prussian grenadiers and fusiliers of Frederick the Great. Meanwhile, in North America, the militiamen of the Thirteen Colonies fighting as 'rangers' had obtained a series of brilliant victories during the French–Indian War. These combat experiences revealed the limits of the line infantry, which had never before been explored: light infantry skirmishers moved much more rapidly than fusiliers on broken terrain and could cause serious losses to the enemy line infantry that advanced in line or column formation. The American Revolution of 1775–83 also highlighted the great tactical flexibility of the light infantry, with the 'minutemen' – so-called due to their supposed ability to be ready to fight at a minute's notice – of the American militias able to defeat the line infantry of the British Army on several occasions thanks to their hit-and-run tactics and superior mobility. France was one of the first European countries to understand the importance of the new light corps; during the Seven Years' War, it had recruited several units of light infantry. These, however, all had only a temporary nature and were disbanded when hostilities

Line infantry officer with winter greatcoat and *surtout* tunic.

Line infantry standard-bearer with the Imperial Eagle of his regiment.

came to an end in 1763. Two decades later, in 1784, the French finally decided to create permanent and regular units of light infantry within their army following the experience gained during the American Revolution. As a result, six regiments of chasseurs were established; these were composite corps of a quite experimental

Grenadier of the
line infantry in
1805.

nature, each of them comprising four companies of light infantry (chasseurs) and four squadrons of light cavalry (chasseurs à cheval). During the Seven Years' War, most of the French light units had been mixed forces of infantry and cavalry that operated as skirmishers or explorers for the regular army. In 1788, understanding that the composite nature of the chasseurs regiments was limiting for both the infantry companies and the cavalry squadrons, it was finally decided to separate the chasseurs from the chasseurs à cheval. The chasseurs were organized into twelve independent battalions: the Chasseurs Royaux du Dauphiné, Chasseurs Royaux de Provence, Chasseurs Royaux Corses, Chasseurs Corses, Chasseurs Cantabres, Chasseurs d'Auvergne, Chasseurs Bretons, Chasseurs des Vosges, Chasseurs des Cevénnes, Chasseurs de Gévaudan, Chasseurs des Ardennes and Chasseurs du Roussillon. As indicated by their official denominations, most of these units were recruited from the border regions of France, where the terrain tended to be mountainous or densely forested. The light infantry recruited from the Alps, the Pyrenees and the island of Corsica were considered to be the best such units. Each of the twelve battalions had a staff and four companies. The staff comprised one lieutenant colonel, one major, one quartermaster, one adjutant, one surgeon-major, one drum-major, four horn players, one master tailor, one master armourer and one master cobbler. Each company had the following composition: one first captain, one second captain, one first lieutenant, one second lieutenant, two sub-lieutenants, one sergeant-major, one quartermaster, four sergeants, eight corporals, eight chosen privates, two drummers and seventy-eight rankers. All the latter were equipped with smoothbore muskets, of the same kind used by the line infantry but produced in a lighter version, except for twelve carabiniers who were armed with rifled carbines and thus acted as sharpshooters.

Following numerous episodes of civil unrest in the countryside, caused by a spate of poor harvests, the local units of the Militia started to be mustered in January 1789 to help prevent the outbreak of a general rebellion. Following the insurrection in Paris in July of that year, the various units of the Militia started to support the revolutionaries politically and thus decided to assume the new denomination of National Guard, their members soon becoming the driving force of the French Revolution and asking for massive reforms in order to improve the living conditions of the peasants. From the outset, service in the new Garde Nationale was much more prestigious than that in the Milice: members of the National Guard mostly came from the middle-classes of the French provinces and were usually commanded by minor aristocrats who were favourable to the reforms demanded by the common people. As National Guardsmen had to provide their own uniform and equipment, within a few months the peculiar peasant character of the old Milice was rapidly substituted by the bourgeoise one of the new Garde Nationale. In July 1790, a year after the outbreak of the revolution, the newly constituted National Assembly of Paris put the National Guard on a more organized footing and decreed that only 'active citizens' (those paying the equivalent of three days of work in taxes) could be admitted to its ranks. During 1789 and 1790, the city of Paris also organized its own units of National Guard, which were particularly numerous from the beginning. Indeed, by the summer of 1790, the infantry of Paris' National Guard comprised a total of sixty battalions (each of which was named after one of the French capital's districts). A single battalion consisted of five companies with 100 guardsmen each, and the sixty battalions were assembled into six divisions of ten battalions each, plus one company of grenadiers and another of chasseurs. The National Guard of Paris quickly became an important political instrument, since it could decisively influence the decisions taken by the National Assembly and the king. Differently from the regular army, the Garde Nationale was a true 'national' military force.

On 1 January 1791, following months of discussions and the analysis of several different projects, the new French parliament finally enacted a complete reform of the French Army. The rank of officer, which had until then been given only to aristocrats, was opened to all citizens regardless of their birth. A new code of military justice was also introduced, the management of the military finances was rationalized and the recruiting operations were placed under the control of the local authorities. The infantry regiments were deeply affected by the reform, losing their traditional titles – most of which had aristocratic origins – and instead being numbered according to their ranking. Only the eleven Swiss regiments were exempt from these changes. Furthermore, the internal composition of individual units was completely modified; while each regiment continued to comprise two battalions, every battalion now had eight companies of fusiliers instead of four. The elite company of grenadiers of each 1st Battalion was retained, while the chasseurs of each 2nd Battalion were transformed into another company of grenadiers. Three months after the reform of the line infantry, the light infantry was also reorganized on 1 April 1791. It continued to be structured on twelve battalions, but the internal organization of its sub-units was modified. Each battalion was now to have eight companies, each of which comprised the following elements: one captain, one lieutenant, one sub-lieutenant, one sergeant-major, two sergeants, one corporal-fourrier, four corporals, four chosen privates, one drummer, six carabiniers and forty rankers. On 21 July that year, the twenty-three foreign infantry regiments were assimilated into the national infantry and thus lost their peculiar features, although the eleven Swiss units, at least on paper, again continued to retain their traditional denominations and codes of law.

Eventually, especially after the royal family was arrested while attempting to flee France, the recently created constitutional monarchy was transformed into a republic,

Uniforms of the line infantry grenadiers (from left to right): grenadier with bearskin, grenadier with 1810 shako and grenadier with 1812 dress.

which caused the outbreak of war with other European nations. As a result, the French parliament started to debate how to increase the number of soldiers in each infantry regiment in the event of a future war mobilization. The political instability that characterized most of 1791 had caused a general increase of desertion rates as well as the outbreak of minor revolts that had severely weakened the discipline of the regular military forces. Consequently, most of the units were understrength and the morale of the regiments was very low due to their new conditions of service, that were seen as inferior to the previous ones. Since both the Provincial Troops and

Grenadier of the line
infantry (left) and
voltigeur of the light
infantry (right).

Militia had been disbanded in March 1791, the new French government had no choice but to use the many units of the National Guard in order to expand its armies. On 3 July 1791, the French parliament authorized the mobilization of forty-five infantry battalions of the National Guard, with a total of 26,000 men. These, known as Gardes Nationales Volontaires, were soon increased to 101,000 when it became clear that the frontiers of France needed to be defended. In August, the new National Guardsmen finally received a proper organization, which had the battalion as its basic unit. The 101,000 volunteers were assembled into battalions of 568 men each, while a single battalion consisted of nine fusilier companies and one grenadier company. The internal establishment of each company was as follows: one captain, one lieutenant, one sub-lieutenant, one sergeant-major, two sergeants, four corporals, one drummer and fifty-two other rank. Each battalion of the National Guard was to have a small staff consisting of two lieutenant colonels, one adjutant-major, one adjutant-NCO, one quartermaster and one armourer. The rankers of each company were to elect their own officers and NCOs; only the adjutant-major and the adjutant-NCO of the battalion's staff were not elected, since they were taken from the line regiments (their main task being to maintain discipline among the inexperienced volunteers). Because the battalions of National Guardsmen were recruited on a local basis, they had a very strong esprit-de-corps, with most of their members bonded by friendship. Eight or ten battalions from the same district could be assembled together in order to form a larger division or legion.

By the outbreak of hostilities with the other European powers, on 20 April 1792, the French regular infantry had been slightly enlarged with the creation of several new units. The line infantry now had 105 regiments, since one had been disbanded and four new ones had been raised. The disbanded unit was the King's Regiment, which had mutinied against the new government. Of the four new line regiments, one was recruited from members of the King's Regiment who swore loyalty to the republic, while the other three were recruited from the best elements of the Paris National Guard. Several of the latter were former royal soldiers of the French Guards Regiment, which had joined the revolutionaries during the first actions of the uprising in the capital in July 1789 before being disbanded. The battalions of light infantry had been expanded too, having been augmented from twelve to fourteen, the two new units being recruited from the best elements of the Paris National Guard. On 24 April 1792, the small section of carabiniers that was included in each battalion of chasseurs was expanded to become a company, and thus each battalion of light infantry started to have nine companies instead of the previous eight. In August 1792, the Swiss Guards Regiment, like the French Guards Regiment before it, was officially disbanded after an angry mob of citizens massacred most of the foreign mercenaries during an attack on the Tuileries Royal Palace.

Soon after the outbreak of war with the other European powers, France faced a military emergency, its territory being attacked from four different directions. The newly constituted republic seemed to be on the verge of collapsing, and its only chance of survival lay in the possibility of recruiting more volunteers to enlarge the ranks of the armies. On 5 May 1792, another forty-five battalions of National Guard were called up and the strength of the existing battalions was increased from 574 to 800 men. In July that year, it was decided that another forty-two battalions would be raised, but the response of the French population to this general call-to-arms was much more enthusiastic than expected by the government: in total, over 275 battalions of national guardsmen were organized across the country, with most of them being rapidly sent to the various fronts.

During the war mobilization of 1792, the French government also strove to increase the number of light infantry units by recruiting more corps of volunteers of a temporary nature, like those that had been organized during the Seven Years' War. These new units were tasked with fighting the so-called Petite Guerre, or Little War, which was to be conducted by using hit-and-run tactics. Between April and May 1792, nine 'legions' of volunteer light infantry were created, each of which consisted of two battalions of chasseurs as well as one regiment of mounted chasseurs and a small detachment of pioneers. In July, a tenth formation of this kind, consisting of eighteen light infantry companies and four light cavalry companies, was formed in the Alps and assumed the name of the Légion du Midi. During the following months, several more units of mixed light infantry and light cavalry were created, frequently comprising foreigners who wanted to fight for the French Republic: some of these gradually became effective fighting forces, while others were of little use once on the battlefield. In addition to the larger legions, a total of 54 compagnies franches, or free companies, with 150 men each were organized, but these small independent corps were soon increased to 140 and were deployed on the various fronts in order to perform a series of auxiliary duties. They proved to be perfect for scouting as well as for skirmishing; their members had a quite irregular character and several of them were dressed in flamboyant uniforms. Over time, however, the most efficient of the free companies started to be consolidated into battalions or legions. As a result, by September 1792, the French irregular light infantry comprised the following units: twelve legions, eight battalions, one half-battalion and 140 companies. The French Army that defeated the Austro-Prussians at the Battle of Valmy, as is clear from the above description, was a very composite force, consisting of regulars who had served in the former Royal Army, middle-class volunteers of the new National Guard

Grenadier of the line infantry (left) and voltigeur of the light infantry (right), both with 1810 shako.

Grenadier of
the line infantry
with winter
greatcoat.

and low-class volunteers of the irregular light infantry companies. The regulars were dressed in their old white royalist uniforms, while the National Guard had 'patriotic' uniforms in the colours of France's new republican flag (red, white and blue) and the light infantry wore exotic uniforms designed according to the personal taste of their commanders. Despite their motley appearance, though, these soldiers were about to surprise the old order.

Chapter 2

The French Infantry from 1793–99

The foreign powers that formed a large military alliance against France in 1792 had been defeated at Valmy because they had underestimated the potential of the new revolutionary army. However, they soon started to pool their full military resources to defeat France, so the republican government of Paris had to find some new solutions to sustain a prolonged war effort. The morale of the regular regiments was still very low, since most of the professional soldiers disliked the new regime; their officers had left France and had organized loyalist military corps that fought on the side of France's enemies. Meanwhile, although the regiments of the National Guard had high morale, they lacked discipline and training. Their officers were inexperienced and they were not used to lengthy military campaigns. Radical reform of the French armed forces was vital, with the two main components of the French Army needing to be amalgamated as soon as possible if the new republican regime was to survive. The solution to this problem was found by Edmond Dubois-Crancé, a French politician, who proposed to replace the regiment as the basic unit of the French infantry. Dubois-Crancé presented a highly intelligent plan to the French parliament, according to which each regular battalion was to be joined by two battalions of National Guardsmen. The new three-battalion regiments derived from this ambitious reform were known as demi-brigades, or half-brigades. Dubois-Crancé's reforms had positive consequences for both the regulars and the volunteers: the former acquired the new patriotic spirit from the National Guardsmen and abandoned their former royalist traditions, while the latter learned drill and discipline from the professional soldiers. The original plan of reform prescribed the creation of 198 demi-brigades, with a total of 594 battalions (198 of regulars and 396 of National Guards). The 1st Half-Brigade, for example, was formed by assembling the 1st Battalion of the 1st Line Infantry Regiment with the two nearest battalions of volunteers (both coming from the same department, if possible). In August 1793, the changes designed by Dubois-Crancé started to be implemented. Each of the new demi-brigades had a staff composed of the following elements: one brigade commander, three battalion commanders, one quartermaster-treasurer, one adjutant-major, one surgeon-major, two aides, three adjutant-NCOs, one drum-major, one drum-corporal, eight drummers, one master tailor, one master cobbler and three master armourers. Each of the three battalions

Uniforms of the line infantry voltigeurs (from left to right): voltigeur in 1804, voltigeurs with 1806 shako and voltigeur with 1812 dress.

of a half-brigade comprised a single company of grenadiers and eight companies of fusiliers. A single company consisted of the following: one captain, one lieutenant, one sub-lieutenant, one sergeant-major, two sergeants, one corporal-fourrier, four corporals, four chosen privates, two drummers and either forty-eight grenadiers or seventy-four fusiliers. Once assembled, the twenty-seven companies that formed a new demi-brigade were mixed so that each battalion had three companies of regulars and six companies of National Guardsmen.

Voltigeurs of the
line infantry with
1812 uniform.

In August 1793, to implement the reform of the army more effectively, the French government took the unprecedented step of declaring a *levée en masse*, or universal levy, whereby all able-bodied and unmarried childless males aged between 18 and 25 were ordered to enlist in the Army, in order to have 300,000 new recruits ready to defend the borders of their country. With the arrival of these conscripts, the 198 demi-brigades that had been planned could be finally organized. Indeed, since the number of new recruits was greater than needed, fifteen surplus 'provisional' half-brigades could also be formed. In January 1794, following the success of his line infantry reorganization, Dubois-Crancé proposed something similar for the light infantry by amalgamating the regular battalions of chasseurs with the light legions of the National Guard and the free companies of irregulars. During 1793, the number of chasseur battalions had already been increased from fourteen to twenty-two by transforming some of the more-disciplined units of volunteers into regular corps. The amalgamation of the light units proved to be slower and more difficult than that of the line formations, but by the beginning of 1795, the French Army could count on a total of thirty-five demi-brigades of light infantry.

In April 1794, each half-brigade was ordered to form an extra company of artillery, which was to be equipped with six 4-pdr guns and would comprise two captains, three lieutenants, six sergeants, one corporal-fourrier, five corporals, one drummer and seventy-five gunners. This measure, however, was not extended to the demi-brigades of light infantry, which were to maintain their higher degree of mobility. By October 1795, thanks to the reforms that had been carried out during the previous two years and to the formation of several new corps, the French Army could deploy an impressive number of infantry units: 205 line infantry demi-brigades de bataille and thirty-five light infantry demi-brigades légère, for a total of 720 battalions. At the end of the eighteenth century, France had the largest population in Europe, but the impressive numbers of its military were mostly the result of the new conscription law that had been introduced in 1793 (no other European power had a recruiting system comparable to that of the French). In November 1795, following the installation of the Directoire as the new government of France, the general structure of French infantry was rationalized and partly reduced: the line infantry could now field 100 half-brigades with some 323,000 men, while the light infantry depoloyed 96,960 soldiers in thirty half-brigades. The size of the light infantry was particularly impressive, especially if compared with those of the other European armies of the time that usually comprised just a few regiments or battalions of light foot troops. In January 1796, the existing infantry units were distributed as follows in the seven regional armies fielded by France: Army of the Sambre and Meuse, twenty-one line and five light half-brigades; Army of the West, sixteen line and six light half-brigades; Army of the Alps, four line and four light half-brigades; Army of the Interior, fourteen line and two light half-brigades; Army of the Rhine and Moselle, twenty-one line and five light half-brigades; Army of Italy, twelve line and six light half-brigades; and Army of the North, twelve line and two light half-brigades.

In October 1798, each of the infantry battalions was required to form a single depot company, and the following September a second such company was formed in each battalion and the six depot companies of each demi-brigade were brought together to form an entire depot battalion. The internal composition of each half-brigade was also slightly modified. The staff of each demi-brigade was now to consist of one brigade commander, four battalion commanders, four adjutant-majors, four adjutant-NCOs, one quartermaster, one postmaster, three medical officers, one drum-major, one drum-corporal, eight musicians, one master tailor, one master cobbler, one master gaiter maker and one master armourer. Each battalion still comprised one elite company of grenadiers and nine companies of fusiliers. The internal establishment of a single company was as follows: one captain, one lieutenant, one sub-lieutenant, one sergeant-major, four sergeants, one fourrier, eight corporals, two drummers and either sixty-four grenadiers or 104 fusiliers. The grenadier companies of each battalion were frequently detached from their demi-brigades in order to form ad hoc temporary battalions of grenadiers, which were used to perform special missions, for example to storm an enemy fortification. Compared with the fusiliers of the line infantry, the chasseurs of the light units were considered to be soldiers of superior quality; it should be remembered, however, that the reforms of 1793–94 had greatly improved the combat capabilities of the French line infantrymen, which had been uneven until then. The patriotic spirit of the volunteers was now common to the whole Army, while the discipline of the old regulars had also been introduced in the ranks of the former National Guardsmen. Many things had changed in just a few years and the French Army had greatly modified its nature, but despite everything it remained a large and effective fighting force during the most chaotic days of the Revolution. The amalgamation of thousands of volunteers into the regular military forces had been a miracle by the organizational standards of the late eighteenth century.

In 1796, Napoleon, the youngest general of the French Army, assumed command of the Army of Italy and started to win a series of brilliant victories over the Piedmontese and Austrians who opposed him in the northern part of the Italian peninsula. On the other fronts where the Republic's armies were deployed, however, the French experienced a series of setbacks and were unable to achieve any significant results. The conflict with the allied powers was gradually becoming a war of attrition and – at least for the moment – the years of the great pitched battles seemed to be over. Unexpectedly, it was Napoleon in Italy who made significant progress. This was

Uniforms of the line infantry voltigeurs: officers (left) and private (right).

against all odds, as his army was only a secondary force that was intended to divert some Austrian troops from the main theatre of operations on the Rhine. The men under the command of the young Corsican general were swiftly able to occupy most of northern Italy, and even to menace Vienna – capital of the Austrian Empire.

The years 1796–99, which saw the Directoire guiding France in a transitional period for the Revolution, were characterized by a series of organizational changes for the French infantry. In September 1798, a new conscription law was introduced, replacing the previous one of 1793 that was starting to cause widespread malcontent among the French people. A general levy could also be called up in case of an emergency, but was very difficult to sustain in the long run since it had disastrous

Sergeant-major of the line infantry voltigeurs wearing 1812 dress in Spain. The brown loose trousers were typical of campaign uniforms.

Officer of the line infantry wearing 1806 experimental white uniform.

consequences for the economy of the country. In addition, France was now on the offensive and was fighting outside its borders: the Republic was no longer in danger, with the French soldiers now exporting the ideals of the Revolution abroad. Consequently, the conscription law of 1798 (introduced by General Jourdan) was based on fair and egalitarian principles, under which all able-bodied citizens aged from 18–30 could volunteer for a period of service in the Army. This would last four years in times of peace or for the entire duration of a campaign in times of war. In addition, all Frenchmen aged between 20 and 25 were liable for military service and could be selected by draft. All the potential conscripts were divided into five annual classes and their names were entered onto a register that was kept in their municipality. Every year, a ballot would draw the number of conscripts required for military service from this register, plus a certain number of conscripts who were placed on a reserve list and had to replace any selected recruit who did not pass the medical examination that took place before their effective admission into the Army. The ballot was drawn from the youngest of the five classes, which was made up of young men aged 20; if more soldiers were needed, the ballot was drawn for a second time from the second of the five classes, and so on. The new recruiting method introduced in 1798 was particularly effective, since it was placed halfway between the royalist system of pre-1789 and the revolutionary one of 1793. The new French Army thus consisted of both professional soldiers who volunteered to serve as well as conscripts who were recruited according to a fair conscription law. Such a system was much more sustainable for the economy and for the society of the state, since it did not damage the productive activities of the people. In late September 1798, a few weeks after the promulgation of the new law, 200,000 new conscripts had already been called up by the government.

The early months of 1799 were a worrying period for France militarily, the Allies obtaining a series of victories over French forces while Napoleon was away from Europe with part of the French Army in Egypt. After Russia joined the anti-French coalition, thousands of Russian soldiers had entered northern Italy to reconquer all the territories that had been lost by the Austrians during the previous years. To deal with the military crisis and have more soldiers at its disposal, the French government decided to call all the five classes of conscripts for the year 1799. At this point, however, the Directoire made a huge organizational mistake, as instead of sending the new conscripts to the various fronts as replacements for the existing units that had suffered serious losses, it organized new independent units with the new recruits. These became known as bataillons auxiliares, or auxiliary battalions, and were intended to operate independently from the existing demi-brigades. Each territorial department organized a certain number of new battalions according to its number of recruits. The new auxiliary battalions comprised ten companies: one of grenadiers, one of chasseurs and eight of fusiliers. No autonomous battalions of light infantry were established. Each company was made up of the following elements: one captain, one lieutenant, one sub-lieutenant, one sergeant-major, four sergeants, one corporal-fourrier, eight corporals, two drummers and 152 men. Individual battalions had a small staff: one battalion commander, one quartermaster-treasurer, one adjutant-major, one surgeon-major, one adjutant-NCO, one drum-major, one master tailor, one master cobbler and one master armourer. The officers of the new battalions were chosen – when possible – from the retired or supernumerary officers who wanted to return to action, while the NCOs were selected half from retired soldiers with some combat experience and half from new conscripts who had good personal capabilities. The Directoire intended the new auxiliary battalions to have a very distinct local nature: being recruited in the various districts of the country, they were made up of men who knew each other very well. The new recruits had very little military experience, but the presence of veteran officers and NCOs was considered sufficient to increase the general quality of these battalions.

In the early months of 1799, France was not only fighting against the Allies on many fronts, but was also experiencing a bloody civil war in its western territories, where a counter-revolution had erupted. The Vandean communities of Catholic peasants had rebelled against the central government and were fighting for the restoration of the monarchy. The Directoire had to send an increasing number of troops to the areas where the rebellion was spreading, which had a negative effect on the course of the war being fought against the Allies. The western departments of France that were involved in the counter-revolution did not recruit any auxiliary battalions like all the other areas, but only auxiliary companies, which were mostly tasked with police duties and remained in their home territory.

The organization of the new bataillons auxiliares was a complete failure, these units revealing their limitations once despatched to the front. Not only did they lack experience, but they did not co-operate well with the existing demi-brigades. As a result, a further reform of the French infantry had to be carried out in order to solve the many problems caused by the military emergency of 1799. The man chosen to implement this new reform was Dubois-Crancé, who was named Minister of War. The French Army was in a deplorable state by the end of 1799: many soldiers were without uniforms and weapons, bread and pay were lacking and morale was low. The only means of survival for most of the French conscripts was to requisition food and clothing from the civilians of the territories on which they were operating. Corruption was rife, many of the officers did nothing to preserve the discipline of the men placed under their command, and there was a general lack of training.

Sergeant of the line
infantry voltigeurs
wearing 1806
experimental white
uniform.

Fusilier of the line infantry wearing 1806 experimental white uniform.

Dubois-Crancé strove to solve the numerous problems as quickly as possible. Firstly, he decided to attach each of the new auxiliary battalions to one of the half-brigades. The bataillons auxiliares were actually transformed into the depot battalions of the demi-brigades, and thus provided replacements for the units that had suffered serious losses during the previous months. All the infirm and wounded soldiers of each half-brigade were transferred to the depot battalions, while the new recruits of the former auxiliary battalions were absorbed into the three active battalions of each half-brigade. The reforms initiated by Dubois-Crancé, which in time had some very positive results, were not completed by him but by General Berthier. On 9 November 1799, Napoleon – who had just returned from his ill-fated Egyptian campaign – staged a military coup and abolished the Directoire. The government of France assumed a new institutional form, that of the Consulate, which consisted of three consuls with special powers, one of whom was Napoleon. The Consulate lasted – at least on paper – until 1804, but Napoleon was soon nominated First Consul and thus assumed a prominent role in the new French government by overshadowing the other two consuls. A few days after the military coup, General Berthier – a personal friend of Napoleon and an officer with incredible organizational skills – replaced Dubois-Crancé and continued his military reforms. Between January and February 1800, the incorporation of the auxiliary battalions into the half-brigades was completed, and thus the French infantry assumed a coherent structure that was much more functional than previously.

Chapter 3

French Infantry Uniforms, 1789–99

The French line infantry of 1789 was uniformed in white, according to the dress regulations of 1779, which had been only slightly modified in 1786. The standard uniform of the line infantry consisted of a black bicorn hat and a white long-tailed coat. The bicorn had an entirely white cockade, which was later replaced with a tricolour one following the abolition of the monarchy. The coat had several elements in the distinctive colour of each regiment: collar, frontal lapels, cuff flaps and piping to the shoulder straps and to the round cuffs. It was worn over a simple white waistcoat and had brass buttons. White trousers were worn together with black gaiters during cold months, and with white gaiters during hot months. The turnbacks of the coat were decorated with fleur de lys badges in the distinctive colour of each regiment, as the lily flower was the symbol of the French royal family. Grenadiers had decorative flaming grenades badges instead of the fleur de lys. On the back of the long-tailed coat there were two three-pointed pocket flaps, placed horizontally, which had only an ornamental function; these were piped in the distinctive colour of each regiment and had three buttons each. The cuff flaps also had three buttons each. The shoulder straps of the fusiliers were white and were piped in the regiment's colour; they were sewn onto the shoulder near the seam of the sleeve and were fixed near the collar by a small brass button. From 1788, the grenadiers received red and fringed epaulettes instead of the normal shoulder straps as a mark of distinction; these elite soldiers would retain them for the following decades. Grenadier companies were easy to recognize because instead of the bicorn hat they wore a dark brown bearskin with a brass plate on the front (bearing the coat-of-arms of the French royal family) and a white plume tipped in the distinctive colour of each regiment on the left side. Wrapped around the headgear there were white decorative cords and flounders. The brass buttons of the coat, both for fusiliers and grenadiers, bore the number of the regiment surrounded by a clasp. The white waistcoat that was worn under the long-tailed coat had a short collar and round cuffs in the distinctive colour of each regiment. Drummers were very easy to recognize on the battlefield, since their coats were dark blue instead of white and were decorated with stripes of lace in the colours of the royal livery.

Sergeant-major of the line infantry voltigeurs wearing 1806 experimental white uniform.

Colonel of the line infantry wearing 1812 uniform.

Fusilier of the line infantry with 1812 dress, including pompom in company colour.

Fusilier of the line infantry with 1812 uniform, including pompom in company colour.

In 1791, the uniform was partially modified, with the black bicorn replaced by a new kind of headgear. This was a casque, or helmet, consisting of a leather skullcap with visor that had a thin brass band to protect the head of the soldier from sabre cuts. The new headgear was decorated with a black bearskin crest and a calfskin headband that was painted to look like leopard-skin. On the left side of the helmet there was a white plume tipped in the distinctive colour of each regiment and a holder made of leather. The plume was worn on parade only, being replaced for daily service with a round woollen tuft in the distinctive colour of the regiment. Below the plume or tuft was a tricolour cockade. As an alternative to the casque, the line infantrymen could wear a *bonnet de police*, or fatigue cap, while serving in their barracks. This was white and had a long triangular cloth *flamme* on the left side. The *bonnet de police* was piped in the regimental colour, and on the front it bore a fleur de lys badge.

The foreign regiments of the French line infantry were uniformed like the national ones, but their coats were in distinctive colours. Of the twelve non-Swiss foreign regiments, nine had sky-blue coats and three had red coats (the three Irish regiments). The eleven Swiss regiments were dressed with white coats like the French ones, but had lapels in a second distinctive colour. The French Guards Regiment and Swiss Guards Regiment, the two major infantry units of the Royal Guard, wore distinctive uniforms. The French Guards were dressed as follows: black bicorn with white cockade and silver external edging, dark blue long-tailed coat with red collar and round cuffs piped in silver, additional silver braiding on the buttonholes of the front of the coat and of the cuffs, red waistcoat with silver frontal piping and silver braiding on the buttonholes, white trousers and white gaiters. The coat of the French Guards did not have frontal lapels but had silver shoulder straps; on the back it had dark blue pocket flaps piped in silver, with silver braiding on the buttonholes. The Swiss Guards Regiment had a black bicorn with white cockade and silver external edging, red long-tailed coat with dark blue collar, lapels and round cuffs piped in silver, additional silver braiding on the buttonholes of the lapels and of the cuffs, white waistcoat, white trousers and white gaiters. The shoulder straps were red with silver piping, while the pocket flaps on the back of the coat were red with silver piping and silver braiding on the buttonholes. The grenadiers of both the French Guards and Swiss Guards had bearskins with silver cords and flounders.

The light infantry chasseurs received their first uniform on 10 August 1784, following their organization. This was similar to that worn by the line infantry but was dark green instead of white, and was also used by the mounted chasseurs. It consisted of the following elements: black bicorn with a tuft of green wool and a white cockade, dark green long-tailed coat with frontal lapels and round cuffs in battalion colour, piping to the collar in battalion colour, dark green shoulder straps piped in battalion colour and having white fringes, chamois waistcoat and breeches, and black or white gaiters. The buttons of the coat were in white metal and bore a hunting horn badge, this symbol being reproduced, in battalion colour, on the back of the coat's turnbacks. Only the left shoulder strap had fringes. The musicians of each regiment were dressed in dark blue like those of the line infantry. With the reorganization of 1786, the infantry chasseurs were separated from the cavalry chasseurs and their uniform was partly modified as follows: black bicorn with a tuft of green wool and a white cockade, dark green long-tailed coat with frontal lapels and round cuffs in battalion colour, piping to the collar in battalion colour, dark green shoulder straps piped in battalion colour, dark green waistcoat and trousers, and black leather half-boots. The footwear was cut to resemble the boots of the light cavalry, having top piping and frontal tassel in battalion colour. The buttons of the coat were in white metal and bore a hunting horn badge, which was reproduced, in battalion colour, on the back of the coat's turnbacks. The chasseurs, like the line infantrymen, had a *bonnet de police* used as a fatigue cap, which was dark green and was piped in battalion colour, having a small woollen tuft in the distinctive colour of each company (scarlet, sky blue, pink and yellow for the 1st to the 4th Company).

In November 1789, after the outbreak of the Revolution, various other minor modifications were introduced, with white metal buttons replaced by brass ones, while the waistcoat and trousers became white. Musicians received a new coat in the distinctive colour of their battalion, decorated with stripes of lace in the colours of the royal livery. On 24 April 1791, the uniforms of the chasseurs were again modified: a hunting horn was added to the battalion number reproduced on the buttons, and a flap with three buttons (piped in the distinctive colour of each battalion) was added to the cuffs. In addition, the light infantry received the new casque headgear that had been introduced for the line infantry. This had a white plume tipped in the battalion colour of each chasseur unit. The carabiniers, or sharpshooters, of each chasseur battalion became easy to recognize thanks to the introduction of two new elements, replacing their black bicorn with a black bearskin (with a red plume as well as white cords and flounders) and substituting their shoulder straps with red fringed epaulettes. The crown placed on the back of the new headgear was red with a white cross. As a result of these changes, the carabiniers started to have the same appearance as the line infantry's grenadiers.

Until September 1791, the newly constituted National Guard did not have a standardized uniform, since it had a distinct militia character and was not a regular military force. From the early months of 1790, however, the National Guardsmen of Paris had started to wear a peculiar dress that could be defined as 'patriotic', since it was produced in the three colours of the future republican flag: white, red and blue. This

Line infantry conscripts during the French campaign of 1814, all wearing the new pokalem fatigue cap.

new uniform, which soon became extremely popular, was undoubtedly influenced by that worn by the French Guards Regiment. Indeed, when the Revolution broke out in Paris during July 1789, this unit of the Royal Guard had joined the insurgents and its members soon became part of the newly created National Guard of Paris. On 27 July 1791, the tricolour uniform was adopted by all the units of the French National Guard, including those from the countryside. It consisted of the following elements: black bicorn with tricolour national cockade and half-white and half-red woollen tuft, dark blue long-tailed coat with red collar and round cuffs piped in white, white frontal lapels piped in red, dark blue shoulder straps piped in red, white turnbacks piped in red, red cuff flaps piped in white, dark blue horizontal pocket flaps on the back of the coat piped in red and having three buttons, brass buttons, white

Grenadier (left) and officer (right) of the line infantry with the provisional uniform worn during the restoration of 1814. Note the use of white cockades instead of the tricolour.

waistcoat, white trousers, and black gaiters during cold months and white gaiters during hot months. Grenadiers had red fringed epaulettes instead of the standard shoulder straps, plus a black bearskin cap as headgear. The bearskin had a tricolour cockade, white cords and flounders, brass frontal plate bearing a flaming grenade and red plume. The distinctive number of each battalion was stamped on the brass buttons of the coat.

The patriotic uniform of the National Guard soon became extremely popular, being recognized as a symbol of the new republican freedom. When the new half-brigades were formed, they usually had one battalion dressed with casque and white coats, while two battalions had bicorn and dark blue coats. They thus without doubt presented a quite motley appearance. On 21 September 1792, the government of the Republic decided to eliminate all symbols of royalty from French military uniforms, and the dress of the regular infantry was modified as follows: all fleur de lys badges were removed, as well as the stripes of lace in the colours of the royal livery that were embroidered on the musicians' uniforms. On 29 August 1793, it was finally decided to adopt the new tricolour uniform of the National Guard as the standard dress of the whole French infantry, with the regulars discarding their helmets and white coats and adopting the same uniform as the volunteers. This was a very important change, since the new patriotic dress introduced for all units in 1793 was to remain the standard uniform of the French infantry until 1812. The helmets and white coats of the former royal regiments were the last connection that the French infantrymen had with their past; with their replacement, the appearance of the French soldiers changed forever. The *habit national*, or national uniform, was also worn by the new auxiliary battalions that were formed to face the military crisis of 1799. It should be remembered, however, that uniformity was not one of the main features of the French Army during the period from 1793–99. Very often, conscripts went to the battlefield dressed in their own civilian clothes, and, since the government was usually very slow to send new pieces of dress to the various military units, it was not uncommon to see regular soldiers wearing non-regulation items of dress like the popular trousers with blue and red vertical stripes.

On 7 September 1793, the light infantry demi-brigades also abandoned their dark green royal uniforms and received a new 'national' dress that was quite similar to that worn by the line infantry. This had three main distinctive features: it was medium blue and not dark blue, its coat was short-tailed and not long-tailed, and its trousers were of the same colour as the coat and not white. The new uniform of the light infantry remained mostly unchanged until 1812, consisting of the following elements: black bicorn with tricolour national cockade and half-green and half-red woollen tuft, medium blue short-tailed coat with red collar and round cuffs piped in white, medium blue frontal lapels, shoulder straps and turnbacks piped in white, red cuff flaps piped in white, medium blue vertical pocket flaps on the back of the coat piped in white and having three buttons, brass buttons, medium blue waistcoat and trousers, and black half-boots with white piping on the top and white tassel on the front. Carabiniers wore the same distinctive elements as the line infantry's grenadiers, with red fringed epaulettes instead of the standard shoulder straps and a black bearskin cap with tricolour cockade, white cords and flounders, red plume and red crown with a white cross. Differently from that of the grenadiers, the bearskin of the carabiniers did not have the brass frontal plate. As the above description makes clear, the uniform of the light infantry was almost entirely medium blue. In addition, due to the fact that it had short tails, it gave its wearer a greater degree of mobility. On 26 October 1801, the uniform of the French light infantry was slightly modified, most notably with the bicorn being replaced by a black shako with black peak, black top and bottom bands, green woollen tuft on the left side, brass rhomboidal badge on the front bearing unit number and national cockade at the base of the tuft. They also wore a medium blue short-tailed coat with red collar and round cuffs piped in white, medium blue frontal lapels piped in white, green fringed epaulettes, medium blue turnbacks piped in white, red cuff flaps piped in white, medium blue vertical pocket flaps on the back of the coat piped in white and having three buttons, brass buttons, red double-breasted waistcoat, medium blue trousers with a red stripe down a buttoned outer stream, and black or white spats worn over black shoes. The carabiniers wore red epaulettes and their shako had red top and bottom bands as well as a red falling plume on the left side. The badges embroidered on the turnbacks were white hunting horns for chasseurs and red flaming grenades for carabiniers. During 1802 and 1803, some small variations were introduced: the shako started to have a new frontal badge bearing the unit number inside a hunting horn as well as decorative cords/flounders (green for chasseurs and red for carabiniers); the tuft/falling plume was replaced by a standing plume (green for chasseurs and red for carabiniers); the green epaulettes of chasseurs started to have red crescents; and the spats were replaced with black half-boots, with piping and tassel in green for chasseurs and in red for carabiniers.

Chasseur of the light infantry with 1793 dress.

Chasseur of the light infantry with 1801 shako.

Chasseur of the light infantry with
1801 shako.

Chapter 4

The Line Infantry, 1800–15

Organization

W hen Napoleon became First Consul of the French Republic in 1799, he inherited a well-organized and quite large contingent of line infantry from the previous revolutionary government, consisting of eighty-six half-brigades with three battalions each. Since by that time the French Republic comprised a total of ninety-six administrative districts, it could be said that almost every district of France provided a demi-brigade of line infantry. The half-brigades were numbered in progressive order from 1 to 99, but there were several vacant numbers: the 31st, 38th, 41st, 49th, 68th, 71st, 83rd, 87th, 90th, 91st, 97th, 98th and 99th. Some of the administrative departments that made up the French Republic, however, were not properly 'French', since they had only recently been annexed by France. There were 18 such departments, which had been established between 1792 and 1798: two in Italy (Chambery and Nice, taken from Piedmont in 1792–93), two in Switzerland, one in southern France (the territory of Avignon, which had previously been part of the Papal States), nine in Belgium (the French annexed the Austrian Netherlands in 1796) and four in Germany (these were located on the right bank of the Rhine and were taken from the Holy Roman Empire). It should be noted, however, that even though these new districts had been conquered from foreign nations, their populations had a distinct French character and thus were easily absorbed into the French nation. By the time of Napoleon's military coup, the designation of demi-brigade de bataille had already been replaced by the new name demi-brigade de ligne, as the separation between line infantry and light infantry had become very clear. After completing the reform that had already been initiated before his rise to power, the First Consul did nothing to change the internal organization of his line infantry units for several years. Each half-brigade continued to consist of three battalions, which by now had a quite homogenous composition in terms of training and experience of their members. A single battalion consisted of one grenadier company and nine fusilier companies; the practice of introducing one artillery company in each demi-brigade had already been discontinued, having been only experimental in nature. A single company consisted of the following elements:

Chasseurs of the light infantry in 1804, all wearing the 1801 shako.

one captain, one lieutenant, one sub-lieutenant, one sergeant-major, five sergeants, one corporal-fourrier, eight corporals, two drummers and 104 privates. The elite grenadier companies had a similar structure, but with four sergeants and sixty-four privates. The staff of each half-brigade comprised one colonel, three battalion commanders, one adjutant, one paymaster, one drum-major, three standard-bearers, one surgeon, four assistant surgeons, one shoemaker, one gaiter maker, one gunsmith, one tailor and eight musicians.

Officer of the light infantry with 1806 shako.

On 24 September 1803, Napoleon decided to replace the term demi-brigade with regiment, a designation that had been used until the reform of 1793. The amalgamation of the regulars with the volunteers had been completed several years before, and there was thus little reason to keep using the old denomination, which was too 'revolutionary' for the First Consul's tastes. The passage from half-brigade to regiment did not affect the numbering of the units, and nor did it introduce any modification of their internal structure. During 1803, however, Napoleon was obliged to intervene in the general structure of his line infantry, with several regiments having to be re-raised following the French defeat in Haiti. The Caribbean island of Haiti was the richest and most flourishing of France's colonies, but since the outbreak of the Revolution a series of revolts by the Haitian slaves (who worked on the profitable plantations of the island) had gradually disrupted French authority. After becoming First Consul, Napoleon did his best to restore order in his Caribbean colony, sending a large expeditionary force to Haiti. Howsever, this force, comprising several demi-brigades de ligne, was practically destroyed by yellow fewer and the rebellious slaves (who received support from Britain). As a result of the terrible defeat suffered in Haiti, which soon became an independent republic, Napoleon had to rebuild the units that had been sent to the island from scratch, and was also able to raise several new regiments: the 100th, 101st, 102nd, 103rd, 104th, 105th, 106th, 107th, 108th, 111th and 112th (the 109th and 110th remained vacant). As a result of this expansion, by 1804, the French line infantry consisted of ninety-seven regiments. During 1803, the artillery company of each active battalion – which had existed only on paper in most cases – was officially abolished. In 1804, Napoleon decided to intervene again with the internal structure of his line infantry battalions by introducing a new category of elite soldiers: the voltigeurs, whose name literally means 'acrobats' and derives from the tactical duties that they had to perform.

Until 1804, unlike the other major European armies, the French Army did not include light infantry companies in its line infantry battalions. The chasseurs were a separate component of the French infantry, and thus had their own autonomous demi-brigades/regiments. Napoleon, who was a great tactician and knew full well how important light infantry was on campaign, decided to change this by including some elite light infantrymen in his line infantry. Napoleon believed that tactically, each infantry battalion needed a certain number of skirmishers to move in open formation in front of the fusilier companies that advanced in either line or column formation. The light skirmishers could explore the terrain in front of their comrades and engage the enemy from a distance by firing – with great accuracy – from covert positions. Scouting and skirmishing were difficult operations, so the soldiers performing them needed special training as well as their own peculiar equipment. The new voltigeurs became the eyes and ears of the line battalions thanks to their superior mobility, which enabled them to advance rapidly on every kind of terrain; it was from this particular feature that the term 'acrobats' came from, since the elite skirmishers were much more flexible than the ordinary line infantrymen. Instead of adding more soldiers to each battalion and in order to retain the standard number of ten companies for each unit, Napoleon ordered that the second company of fusiliers in each line infantry battalion retrain its members in order to become a voltigeur company. These were an elite sub-unit, like the grenadier company that was already included in each battalion. As a result, from 1804, each line infantry battalion started to have two elite companies and eight fusilier companies.

The creation of the voltigeurs was not a completely new move, since the auxiliary battalions that had been created some years before already included one company of chasseurs. It was Napoleon, however, who extended this temporary measure to all the line units of the French Army. The new voltigeurs soon became skilled at sharpshooting, receiving specific training in marksmanship and learning how to fire from cover. Over time, the voltigeur companies started to be detached – quite frequently – from their parent battalions in order to form temporary ad hoc battalions of elite skirmishers. These were employed to conduct special operations, such as storming enemy positions or conducting long-range scouting missions. When a line infantry battalion was deployed in line on the battlefield, the grenadier company was placed on the right and the voltigeur company on the left of its formation; as a result, the two elite companies were also known as flank companies to differentiate them from the centre companies of fusiliers. Thanks to their superior mobility, the voltigeurs could also cooperate effectively with the cavalry, as they could support mounted skirmishers with their accurate fire. Generally speaking, the grenadiers were chosen from the tallest and strongest recruits assigned to each battalion, with the voltigeurs selected from the smallest men since they had to move very rapidly. In addition, both grenadiers and voltigeurs usually had some combat experience, because they were chosen from veterans who had already served for several years.

After 1804, the general structure of the French line infantry saw no significant changes until 1808: these were the years of Napoleon's greatest victories and of the proclamation of the French Empire. The French line infantry showed their valour to great effect in a series of memorable pitched battles: the victories at Ulm, Austerlitz, Jena, Auerstadt, Eylau and Friedland. The 1805 campaign against Austria, in particular, was a perfect example of how Napoleon employed his line regiments in a very innovative way. By moving faster than their enemies and living off what the territory could offer them, the French infantrymen could cover enormous distances in just a few days and thus could surprise their enemies with audacious outflanking manoeuvres that gave them a precious local superiority. The French fusiliers were well-disciplined and could adapt to any tactical situation; they did not flinch from launching frontal bayonet assaults, but they also knew how to fight in line by firing their muskets from short distance. They were used to any possible kind of

personal sacrifice and showed incredible endurance. Furthermore, their company officers were intelligent and audacious, having obtained their ranks thanks to their personal capabilities, while the backbone of the regiments was the veteran NCOs, who were an example to follow for the rankers.

On 18 February 1808, Napoleon modified the organization of his line infantry by enlarging it significantly but without creating any new regiments. Under his latest reforms, each line infantry regiment consisted of four active battalions – known as bataillons de guerre – plus one depot battalion, the latter having a smaller establishment than the others since it consisted of just four fusilier companies. A single bataillon de guerre comprised one company of grenadiers, one company of voltigeurs and four companies of fusiliers. Consequently, a line infantry regiment had four companies of grenadiers, four companies of voltigeurs, sixteen companies of fusiliers and four depot companies. The depot units were mostly tasked with providing new recruits to the bataillons de guerre as replacements. The staff of each regiment now consisted of the following elements: one colonel, one major, four battalion commanders, five adjutants, five assistants, ten sergeant-majors, three standard-bearers, one drum-major, one drum-corporal, one bandmaster, seven musicians, four craftsmen, one quartermaster, one paymaster, one surgeon-major and four assistant surgeons. A single company comprised one captain, one lieutenant, one sub-lieutenant, one sergeant-major, four sergeants, one corporal-quartermaster, eight corporals, two drummers and 121 privates. The grenadier and voltigeur companies had this standard internal establishment too. Grenadiers were chosen from soldiers who had four years of service and had participated in at least two of the following battles:

Carabinier of the light infantry in 1806.

Uniforms of the light infantry carabiniers (from left to right): carabinier with busby hat, carabiniers with bearskin, carabiniers with 1806 shako and carabinier with 1812 uniform.

Ulm, Austerlitz, Jena and Friedland. A grenadier also had to be at least 173.5cm tall. Voltigeurs were selected from soldiers with two years of service, and they could not be taller than 150cm. Both the grenadiers and voltigeurs received higher pay than the fusiliers due to their elite status. The depot battalion was commanded by a major and was not sent to the front in case of war. Each of its four companies had a different function: the 4th Company never left the depot and was mostly tasked with dressing and training the new recruits (for this reason it was assisted by a dressing captain and a quartermaster-treasurer); the 1st Company and 3rd Company were responsible for transferring the newly trained recruits to the active battalions; and the 2nd Company was generally employed to perform garrison duties in the various military facilities. Attached to the 4th Company were the so-called *enfants de troupe* – sons or orphans of soldiers who were on the battalion's payroll – and the veteran soldiers who were awaiting retirement or pensioning. The four bataillons de guerre of each regiment included four sapeurs (pioneers) each, who were attached to the grenadier company and were under command of a pioneer corporal (there was one such NCO for each regiment). The sappers acted as combat engineers, their main task being to build field fortifications as well as to remove any obstacle that could be encountered by the battalion during its march. They had the same formal status and privileges as the grenadiers.

Musicians were a fundamental component of Napoleon's line infantry, since it was they who transmitted the orders of officers to the rank and file in the chaos of battle. Most of the line infantry musicians were young boys, orphans or sons of soldiers, who earned a living by being part of the Army. Grenadier and fusilier companies had drummers, while voltigeur companies had cornet players due to their light infantry character. The musicians of the regimental staff had a special status compared with those of the regular companies, symbolizing the martial spirit and traditions of the regiment and marching at the head of it during parades, so they wore extravagant uniforms, enjoyed a series of privileges and were commonly known as the 'head of the column'. The drum-major, the leader of all the musicians of a regiment, was usually a veteran of many campaigns and thus had a special relationship with his younger comrades. Of all the musicians of a regiment, he usually had the most ornate dress. Standard-bearers were another important component of the regimental staff; one of them had the honour to carry the Imperial Eagle of his regiment on the battlefield. The Imperial Eagle, like that of the ancient Roman legions, was a symbol of the soldiers' loyalty towards their emperor, and was therefore the most precious possession of each regiment. Losing an Eagle in battle was a disaster that could destroy the reputation of a regiment. The importance of an Imperial Eagle was so great that the other two standard-bearers of a regiment escorted the senior standard-bearer who had the honour to carry the standard.

The internal organization of the French line infantry units introduced in 1808 remained practically unchanged until the end of the Napoleonic Period in 1815. However, during these years, the general establishment of the French infantry continued to be increased with the formation of many new units. Several of the existing regiments added a 5th, 6th or even a 7th Battalion to their four bataillons de guerre. Napoleon could also create new regiments thanks to the territorial expansion of his empire. The first of these new units to be created was the 113th Regiment, which came into existence in May 1808, formed by converting an infantry regiment from Tuscany into a French line unit. Since 1801, the Grand Duchy of Tuscany, one of the many Italian states, had been transformed by the French into a puppet state known as the Kingdom of Etruria, which had a small army that comprised a single infantry regiment of good quality. In December 1807, Napoleon decided to absorb the Kingdom of Etruria into the French Empire, and this unit became part of the French line infantry as the new 113th Regiment. In 1807, in view of his invasion of Spain, Napoleon organized seven provisional regiments of line infantry from new recruits, and after the initial conquest of the Iberian peninsula in 1808, these were transformed into permanent units and absorbed into the French line infantry (becoming the 114th, 115th, 116th, 117th, 118th, 119th and 120th Regiments). On 20 March 1807, in order to create a military reserve that could be employed to defend the frontiers of his empire while he was fighting away from France, Napoleon ordered the formation of the so-called légions de réserve de l'intérieur, or reserve legions of the interior. There were five in total and they had their bases in Lille, Metz, Rennes, Versailles and Grenoble. Each of the five legions consisted of four line infantry companies and thus was numerically comparable to a battalion. According to Napoleon's original plans, the reserve legions were not to operate outside the borders of France, but three of them were sent to fight in Spain during the latter part of 1807. As a result, in January 1809, the five légions de réserve de l'intérieur were absorbed into the regular line infantry and became the following units: the 121st Regiment (raised from the 1st and 2nd Reserve Legion) and 122nd Regiment (raised from the 3rd, 4th and 5th Reserve Legion).

In 1810, the Kingdom of Holland – which had been ruled by Napoleon's brother, Louis Bonaparte, as a puppet state of France since 1806 – was annexed to the French Empire, with its armed forces absorbed into the French Army. Thanks to the incorporation of the Dutch infantry units, the French line infantry could raise the 123rd, 124th, 125th and 126th Regiment during 1810. The 126th Regiment was disbanded in 1813 and its members were absorbed into the 123rd Regiment. In 1811, another two units were added to the French line infantry by converting three corps of Honour Guards (ceremonial units made up of middle-class volunteers from the largest cities of the empire) into regular units: the Honour Guards of Hamburg and Lubeck became the 127th Regiment, while the Honour Guards of Bremen became the 128th Regiment. In 1811, the new 129th Regiment was created from soldiers of the German states of Oldenburg and Westphalia, parts of which were annexed to France. In 1809, in order to have more infantry units available to fight in Spain, Napoleon formed seven temporary auxiliary battalions by gathering together various detachments of line infantry regiments that were serving in the Iberian peninsula. In 1811, these battalions created two new regular

Uniforms of the light infantry (from left to right): carabinier, chasseur and voltigeur.

Uniforms of the light infantry (from left to right): sergeant-major of the voltigeurs, voltigeur with busby hat, voltigeur with shako and chasseurs with shako.

regiments (one of line infantry and one of light infantry). The 1st, 3rd and 6th Auxiliary Battalions became the 130th Line Regiment, while the 2nd, 4th, 5th and 7th Auxiliary Battalions became the 34th Light Regiment. Another three line infantry regiments – the 131st, 132nd and 133rd – were created in 1811. The first two were made up of French conscripts, while the third was obtained by converting an existing unit of Italian conscripts. On 8 June 1808, following the annexation of Tuscany to the French Empire, Napoleon ordered the organization of a new battalion made up of conscripts from the new Italian departments which had resisted conscription. This semi-penal unit had a light infantry character from its foundation and became a regiment in 1810 (with five battalions). Its official denomination was the 1st Mediterranean Regiment. In March 1811 a 2nd

Mediterranean Regiment of the same kind was created, but this was soon absorbed into the French line units as the 133rd Regiment.

Following the disastrous Russian campaign of 1812, despite having suffered enormous losses, Napoleon continued to expand his line infantry by creating new regiments. In January 1813, the 134th Regiment was formed from the recently disbanded Garde de Paris, which will be covered in full detail in another chapter. During 1813, in order to face the Allies in Germany with a sufficient number of soldiers, the emperor had no choice but to use the National Guard – which had lost most of its previous importance since the glory days of the Revolution. Several units of the National Guard – which was now organized on cohorts that had the same strength as the previous battalions – were banded together to form a large number of new line regiments. Each department of the empire had to provide a cohort of infantry to the National Guard, which could thus potentially muster many thousands of men. The following new units were created in 1813 from the cohorts of various districts: the 135th, 136th, 137th, 138th, 139th, 140th, 141st, 142nd, 143rd, 144th, 145th, 146th, 147th, 148th, 149th, 150th, 151st, 152nd, 153rd, 154th, 155th and 156th. The large number of new units that were organized during 1813 and 1814 were not of the same quality as those from before the Russian campaign, in most cases consisting of National Guardsmen or recruits who were too young to have any military experience. The French conscripts of 1814 was called the Marie-Louises by the veteran soldiers returning from Russia, since they were seen as being too young to have a beard, although the expression also came from the fact that it had been Napoleon's young wife, Marie-Louise, who issued the decrees of October 1813 that ordered the raising of 280,000 new conscripts. For the first time since the introduction of the 1798 laws regarding recruiting, conscription was extended to young men aged just 18. France was under threat of a foreign invasion, so every able-bodied man was needed to defend *la patrie*. The conscripts of 1813 and 1814 received only superficial training lasting just two weeks before being sent to the front, but they nevertheless fought with great courage to defend their homeland during the French campaign of 1814. They were short of uniforms, equipment and weapons, and were in addition not used to the harsh conditions that were typical of a winter campaign. The minimum required age for conscription had been reduced from 20 to 19 years on 19 December 1806, but until the autumn of 1813 those aged 18 had never been conscripted. The decrees promulgated by Empress Marie-Louise thus came as a real shock for most French families.

After the first abdication of Napoleon, on 12 May 1814, the restored monarchy greatly reduced the number of line infantry regiments of the French Army. All the new units – numbered from 113–156 – that had been created between 1808 and

1814 were disbanded, along with several other regiments, in order to bring the total number of line infantry units down to ninety. With the adoption of this new structure, all the regimental numbers that had remained vacant until then were used, and thus the line infantry units were numbered from one to ninety without any gaps. When Napoleon returned to France from his exile on Elba in February 1815, he did not change the new general structure of ninety line infantry regiments, but restored the old numeration, which had been inherited from the Revolutionary Period and thus had a certain ideological importance for the units. Generally speaking the reduction ordered by the restored monarchy in 1814 had some positive effects, since by axing the most inexperienced regiments, the remaining ninety could fill their ranks with the best elements of the disbanded units. Consequently, the line infantry regiments commanded by Napoleon at Waterloo in 1815 were of better quality compared with those of 1814.

Uniforms and equipment

In 1799, the French line infantrymen were still dressed in the national uniform that had been introduced in 1793: black bicorn with national cockade having orange-yellow lace holder and red-over-white pompom made of wool, dark blue long-tailed coat with brass buttons and white frontal lapels piped in red, dark blue shoulder straps piped in red, red collar piped in white, red round cuffs piped in white, white cuff flaps piped in red, white turnbacks piped in red, horizontal pocket flaps on the back of the coat piped in red and having three buttons, white waistcoat, white trousers, black gaiters during cold months or white gaiters during hot months, plus black shoes. This was the standard dress of the fusiliers. The grenadiers had a different headgear, a black bearskin with brass frontal plate bearing a flaming grenade, red crown on the back with a white cross, red plume on the left side with a national cockade at its base, red decorative cords and flounders, and black leather peak. They also wore a dark blue long-tailed coat with brass buttons and white frontal lapels piped in red, red fringed epaulettes, red collar piped in white, red round cuffs piped in white, white cuff flaps piped in red, white turnbacks piped in red and having decorative red flaming grenades embroidered on them, horizontal pocket flaps on the back of the coat piped in red and having three buttons, white waistcoat, white trousers, black gaiters during cold months or white gaiters during hot months, and black shoes. Over time, a few features of this uniform were slightly modified: the tails of the coat became shorter in order to be more practical, while the frontal lapels started to have an accentuated curve. According to official dress regulations, the collar and cuffs had to be red with white piping, but it was not uncommon to see white collar and cuffs with red piping.

Uniforms of the light infantry (from left to right): chasseurs with greatcoat, officer of the voltigeurs and officer of the chasseurs.

Sapper of the
light infantry
carabiniers with
axe and white
leather apron.

Dark blue cuff flaps with red piping were also quite common, and sometimes the cuff flaps were completely absent from the coat. These variations derived from the fact that uniforms were produced on a local basis, but became much rarer since Napoleon did his best to dress his soldiers appropriately. Other non-regulation modifications included the lack of red piping to the frontal lapels and the use of vertical pocket flaps on the back of the coat (instead of the horizontal ones prescribed by regulations). The decorative badges embroidered on the white turnbacks of the tails were present with some regularity only on the uniforms of grenadiers, whereas fusiliers mostly did not have them or displayed a huge variety of different badges such as stars, eagles, diamonds or hearts. After 1804, eagle badges became the most popular.

The black bicorn hat, the standard headgear of the French line infantry, was worn in two different positions, according to the activities that its wearer was performing: when worn across the head (*en bataille*), its wearer was ready to fight, but when worn fore-and-aft (*en colonne*), its wearer was marching. Pompoms gradually replaced the previous tufts made of wool, and were usually half-red and half-white; as time progressed, however, the colour of the pompom started to be different for each fusilier company of a battalion and thus became a mark of distinction. Grenadiers wore their massive bearskins on campaign and on parade, but could use the standard bicorn on other occasions. Sometimes, the cords and flounders of the bearskin could be white instead of red. Both the fusiliers and grenadiers also used the *bonnet de police* undress cap, which was dark blue with red piping and had a tasselled stocking end folded up and tucked behind the right-hand side of the stiffened headband. The tassel was red, while on the front of the cap there was a red flaming grenade for grenadier companies. When not in use, the *bonnet de police* was rolled and strapped under the cartridge box of each soldier.

According to the egalitarian principles of the Revolution, officers were dressed exactly like their men, although their uniforms were of finer material. The lace holder of the bicorn's cockade was golden for officers. They also wore a gilt gorget under their neck, which was mostly used on parade and was made of decorative silver that usually included unit number and – after 1804 – an Imperial Eagle. The gorget was the last remnant of the medieval knight's armour, a symbol of high military status. Officers showed their rank on their uniforms thanks to gold lace epaulettes that were worn on the shoulders. These were designed according to a general scheme that had been introduced in 1786 and remained valid after the Revolution. Each rank corresponded to a different combination of epaulettes: colonels had epaulettes with the larger bullion fringes on both shoulders; majors had epaulettes with bullion fringes but with silver straps; battalion commanders had bullion fringes only on the left epaulette; captains had gold lace fringes only on the left epaulette; adjutants had gold lace fringes only on the right epaulette; lieutenants had them like captains but with one red stripe on the straps; sub-lieutenants had them like captains but with two red stripes on the straps; and adjutant-NCOs had red straps with two golden stripes and mixed red-and-gold fringes only on the left epaulette. While on active service, officers frequently replaced their coat with a single-breasted tunic without lapels known as a *surtout*, or overall. This was entirely dark blue, with red piping to the collar, front and round cuffs. Like the coat, however, it had the epaulettes showing rank on the shoulders. An NCO's rank was shown by diagonal bars of lace that were applied on the lower sleeves: two orange-yellow bars for corporals, one golden bar piped in red for sergeants, two golden bars piped in red for sergeant-majors. Both NCOs and rankers had lace service chevrons on the upper sleeves of their coats, which were worn point uppermost and were golden for senior NCOs and red for junior NCOs or rankers. The number of chevrons corresponded to the years of service: one for ten years of service, two for fifteen years and three for twenty years.

When the voltigeurs were introduced in 1804, they received a distinctive uniform: black bicorn with national cockade having orange-yellow lace holder and green pompom surmounted by a yellow brush, dark blue long-tailed coat with brass buttons and white frontal lapels piped in red, green epaulettes with yellow crescent, yellow collar piped in red, red round cuffs piped in white, white cuff flaps piped in red, white turnbacks piped in red with yellow hunting horns embroidered on the back, horizontal pocket flaps on the back of the coat piped in red and having three buttons, white waistcoat, white trousers, black gaiters during cold months or white gaiters during hot months, and black shoes. From the beginning, yellow became the distinctive colour of the voltigeurs, like red was that of the grenadiers. All the line infantrymen wore loose trousers during most of their daily life, and closer-fitting breeches on campaign or on parade. While in their barracks, the NCOs and rankers usually wore only their white waistcoats, which were long-sleeved and single-breasted. These could sometimes have a red collar and round cuffs, something that was not prescribed in official regulations. The waistcoats slowly started to be worn also as campaign dress, especially during hot months in the Mediterranean regions. The waistcoat had two horizontal pocket flaps on the front and two brass buttons on each cuff. When wearing it on campaign, grenadiers and voltigeurs added their distinctive epaulettes to the waistcoat. Until 1805, for winter use, the line infantrymen did not receive greatcoats produced by the Army and thus had to wear their own civilian overcoats or cloaks. During 1805 and 1806, greatcoats were issued to most of the regiments for the first time; these were usually single-breasted, but could also be double-breasted. Their colour was not standardized, ranging from beige to brown,

Officers of the light infantry (from left to right): officer with shako, officers with busby hat and officer with 1812 uniform.

while grey examples were also quite common. The greatcoats of officers were usually dark blue. The same epaulettes, rank bars and service chevrons worn on the coat were applied on the greatcoat.

In February 1806, there was an important modification in the uniforms of the French line infantry, with the fusiliers and voltigeurs replacing their bicorn with a shako. The latter headgear was distributed to the whole line infantry in 1806 and 1807, and quickly became popular. It had a body made of black felt or board, which widened slightly towards the top, and a waterproofed crown. Around the top and the bottom of the shako there were leather reinforcement bands, while on the front

Chasseur
of the light
infantry with
1812 dress.

there was a leather peak. A leather chevron was usually applied as strengthening on each side of the shako. On the front of the top band there was a tricolour cockade placed above a lozenge-shaped brass plate that bore an embossed Imperial Eagle and the number of the regiment. The shako was kept in position by brass chinscales that consisted of circular bosses; the first boss on each side, applied on the bottom band of the headgear, was larger than the others and bore a decorative badge (a five-pointed star for fusiliers, flaming grenade for grenadiers and hunting horn for voltigeurs). Above the cockade there was a woollen pompom for fusiliers and a plume for grenadiers and voltigeurs. The pompom was in company colour, while the plume of grenadiers was red and that of voltigeurs was yellow with a green tip. Wrapped around the shako were decorative cords and flounders, which were usually removed while on campaign; these were white for fusiliers, red for grenadiers and green for voltigeurs. The shakos of the officers had gold lace on the top band, golden cords and flounders, golden lace holder for the cockade and gilded fittings. Sappers were dressed like grenadiers, but with a few differences: they had a distinctive badge, consisting of two crossed axes, embroidered in red or white on the sleeves, and the frontal plate of their bearskin did not have the flaming grenade of the grenadiers. The sappers carried several special pieces of equipment: white leather gauntlets, white leather apron and white leather axe-case. Beards were mandatory for sappers, and were extremely popular too among grenadiers.

On 25 April 1806, Napoleon decided to change the basic colour of the line infantry uniforms from dark blue to white, reverting back to the traditional dress of the pre-revolutionary French foot troops. This decision was mostly taken for economic reasons: as a result of Great Britain's naval blockade of continental Europe, the French found themselves cut off from all the major sources of supply of indigo, the key ingredient of the dyes that were used to produce the dark blue cloth of the line infantry uniforms. Initially, the French Ministry of War tried to find domestic substitutes for indigo, but these proved to be inefficient and very expensive. Consequently, the emperor started considering the possibility of changing the basic colour of the uniforms; after extensive research, white was chosen as the cheapest alternative to dark blue. On 13 February 1805, Napoleon authorized the trial use of new white uniforms in the third battalions of two infantry regiments: the 18th Line Regiment and the 4th Light Regiment. The emperor was satisfied with the results of the trial, and thus – on 25 April 1806 – he decreed the adoption of the new white coats for his entire line infantry, starting with the following regiments: the 3rd, 4th, 8th, 12th, 14th, 15th, 16th, 17th, 18th, 19th, 21st, 22nd, 24th, 25th, 27th, 28th, 32nd, 33rd, 34th and 36th. Under Napoleon's plans, the process of re-uniforming his line infantry was to be completed by 1809. The new dress regulations of 1806 introduced an elaborate system for identifying each regiment by using a unique pattern of coloured facings and piping. For this purpose, the line infantry regiments were divided into fourteen groups, with eight units in each. Each group was assigned a distinctive facing colour (from the first to the last, in progressive order): dark green, black, scarlet, dark brown, violet, sky blue, pink, light orange, dark blue, yellow, grass green, madder red, crimson and iron grey. Within each of the fourteen groups, the first four regiments had yellow metal buttons and horizontal pockets on the back of their coats, while the second four regiments had white metal buttons and vertical pockets on the back of their coats. The units within each of these series of four were differentiated according to the following system: the first wore the distinctive colour on lapels, collar and cuffs; the second wore it on lapels and cuffs; the third wore it on lapels and collar; and the fourth wore it on collar and cuffs. Any facing left white was trimmed in the distinctive colour, while all the facings in the distinctive colour were piped in white. The complex system of specifications described above was followed quite closely in the manufacturing of the new uniforms, which retained the same basic cut as the dark blue ones, as well as the distinctive elements prescribed for grenadiers and voltigeurs. The shako was not modified. In the end, however, only twelve of the twenty regiments that had been selected to receive the new dress actually replaced their dark blue uniforms with the white ones. The opposition of the officers and other ranks to the introduction of the new dress was very strong, as the French line infantrymen had always been proud of their blue uniforms. White was the colour of the old – and hated – royal army, as well as of the Austrian infantry (enemies for decades of the French soldiers).

The critical test of the new white uniform came soon after its adoption by the first twelve regiments, and against Napoleon's expectations, it ended in failure. During the Prussian campaign of 1806 and Polish campaign of 1807, the white coats proved impossible to keep clean. In action, any blood showed up vividly on them, which had important negative consequences for the morale of the wearer, while on the march, the white coats were soon covered with dust and mud. In addition, the new uniforms soiled so easily that they were also uneconomical; the old dark blue coats were more expensive to produce than the white ones, but they had the merit of being durable. As a result of all these matters, the emperor halted the distribution of the new dress on 23 May 1806, and in October that year he ordered production of dark blue coats to be resumed. The grand plan for re-uniforming the French line infantry had been a complete failure, mainly due to the opposition of the soldiers who loved their national dress, but also because of several practical reasons. It should be noted, however, that the regiments that had already received the new white uniforms were

Drum-major (left) and drummers (right) of the line infantry. Some of the musicians are wearing the *bonnet de police* fatigue cap.

Musicians of a line infantry unit's regimental band in their brightly coloured uniforms.

ordered to continue using them until they wore out, so the French line infantry continued to include some regiments dressed in them until 1809.

The dark blue uniforms of the French line infantry remained unchanged until 9 November 1810, when a new model of shako was introduced that was slightly taller and more robust than the previous one, and did not have chevrons on the sides nor cords or flounders. The cords and flounders, however, continued to be worn by most of the regiments. The new shako was intended to have a pompom for grenadiers and voltigeurs instead of the plume, but this feature was never adopted: the grenadiers simply added a red pompom to the base of their red plumes, while the voltigeurs received a yellow pompom at the base of their yellow and green plumes. The frontal plate of the new shako was lozenge-shaped and bore the distinctive number of each regiment. However, several units used a different brass plate that was crescent-shaped and bore an Imperial Eagle. This alternative design, which was not prescribed by official regulations, became so popular that it was officially adopted with the new dress regulations of 1812. In February 1811, the system of pompoms and plumes for the headgear was regularized as follows: colonels had an entirely white plume, with majors having a white-over-red plume, battalion commanders an entirely red plume, and all other officers and NCOs of the regimental staff a white pompom. Grenadiers had a red pompom, and voltigeurs a yellow one. Each of the four fusilier companies of a line infantry battalion wore pompoms in a different colour: dark green for the 1st Company, sky blue for the 2nd Company, orange for the 3rd Company and violet for the 4th Company. Sometimes the pompom could bear battalion number in white and be surmounted by a tuft in the same colour, but these variations were not permitted according to official dress regulations. On the new shako introduced in 1810, the golden top band worn by officers had a different width according to rank.

Despite all the successive dress regulations, on campaign the 'perfect' uniforms described in the previous paragraphs had a quite different appearance, as the harsh conditions of life for the common soldiers had a direct impact on their clothing. Loose trousers or overalls were extremely common, and could be grey, ochre, brown or dark blue according to the materials that were available locally. Shako covers were used by most of the soldiers in order to protect their precious headgear; these were made of black waterproof fabric or buff cotton. The covers concealed most of the shako's decorations, except for the pompom or plume. Sometimes, regimental numbers or badges could be painted on the front of these covers. During long marches, the trousers were turned up at the bottom or were tied around the ankle with string, while the greatcoat was frequently worn directly over the waistcoat and the dark blue coat was carried in the knapsack.

The uniforms of the musicians were governed, until the 1812 dress regulations, by the personal tastes of the colonels commanding individual regiments. Members of the regimental band wore coats in extravagant colours, like red or yellow, which sometimes had an 'exotic' flavour, quite frequently worn with non-regulation headgears like bicorns adorned with ostrich-feathers or *czapkas* (square-topped cavalry caps, typical of the Polish lancers). The uniforms of the regimental bandsmen were a riot of colours: their facings were all trimmed with multi-colour lace, they had trefoil-shaped epaulettes in the same colour as the trimming and sometimes had decorative shoulder wings that were worn under the epaulettes. Trousers could be decorated on the front with embroidered knots, while the standard footwear was usually replaced with black leather half-boots having coloured top edging and frontal tassel. Plumes, pompoms, cords and flounders of the shakos could be in many different colours (usually matching that of the coat or the trimming). Drum-majors had the most ornate uniforms, usually with a black bicorn trimmed with golden lace and massive plumes (usually in the three national colours of France). They also had leather gauntlets and a laced baldric made of cloth to support their ornamental sabrer, but their most important mark of distinction was the corded mace that was used to direct the regimental band. In most cases, the trimming of the drum-majors' uniforms was in gold, like the epaulettes that they wore on the shoulders. As an alternative to the bicorn, these veteran musicians could have a busby made of fur that was very similar to that worn by the contemporary French light cavalry. Drum-corporals were dressed similarly to drum-majors, but with less decorations. The musicians of the individual companies – drummers for fusiliers, fifers for grenadiers and horn players for voltigeurs – were dressed in a much simpler way and looked more or less like their comrades. They had coloured lacing on the facings, the pockets and the turnbacks, and in addition they usually had decorative stripes of coloured lace applied on the sleeves and coloured shoulder-wings. Shako ornaments, company distinctions, badges on the turnbacks and epaulettes were all the same as the ordinary soldiers.

On 19 January 1812, new dress regulations were introduced for the French infantry. These, which remained in use until the definitive fall of Napoleon in 1815, were named after a Major Bardin who was responsible for their issue. They retained the general features and colours of the blue national uniform used until then, but introduced some important modifications. For example, the old coat was replaced with a double-breasted and short-tailed dark blue jacket known as a *habit-veste*. This had plastron-style lapels on the front and vertical pockets on the back. The white short turnbacks of the new uniform bore a dark blue crowned 'N' for fusiliers, a red flaming grenade for grenadiers and a yellow hunting horn for voltigeurs. Fusiliers had dark blue shoulder straps piped in red, while grenadiers had red epaulettes and

Musician of a line infantry unit's
regimental band, with *czapka* headgear.

Musician of a line infantry unit's regimental
band, with *czapka* headgear.

Horn player of a line infantry voltigeur company. Note the additional yellow trimming to the facings and the red shoulder wings.

voltigeurs yellow epaulettes with green crescents (this did not change from the previous uniform). Rank distinctions and service chevrons remained unchanged. The white waistcoat, which was no longer visible, now had a lower collar and coloured shoulder straps (dark blue for fusiliers, red for grenadiers and yellow for voltigeurs). The black or white gaiters no longer extended over the knee. The 1812 dress regulations also introduced a new model of shako, with a different brass frontal plate that bore a crowned Imperial Eagle atop a semi-circular plate into which the regimental number was cut. The new shako had decorative brass finials, which reproduced a lion's head for fusiliers, a flaming grenade for grenadiers and a hunting horn for voltigeurs. The tricolour cockade and brass chinscales of the previous model of shako were retained, and although cords and flounders were officially abolished, in practice they continued to be worn by most of the regiments. The bearskins of the grenadiers fell out of use, and thus grenadier companies also started to wear shakos. Grenadiers' shakos had red top and bottom bands, as well as red side-chevrons, whereas voltigeurs had yellow top and bottom bands as well as yellow side-chevrons on their shakos. The shakos of the fusiliers had a tufted pompom in company colours, while those of the elite companies had a tufted pompom and plume in red for grenadiers and a green tufted pompom and green plume tipped in yellow for voltigeurs. The Bardin Regulations also introduced a new model of forage cap that replaced the previous *bonnet de police*; this was known as a pokalem and was a pie-shaped dark blue cap with a folding neck-flap that could be fastened under the chin. The pokalem was piped in red and bore the regimental number or the grenadier or voltigeur badge embroidered in red on the front.

As a result of all the changes described above, the new uniform of a fusilier as stipulated by the 1812 dress regulations was as follows: black shako with black top and bottom bands, brass chinscales and frontal plate, national cockade and pompom in company colour; dark blue *habit-veste* with red collar and round cuffs piped in white, dark blue shoulder straps piped in red, dark blue cuff flaps piped in red, white frontal plastron piped in red, brass buttons, white short turnbacks piped in red with embroidered company badge, dark blue vertical pocket flaps piped in red on the back of the jacket; white trousers; and black or white gaiters. Grenadiers had plume, pompom, side-chevrons, and top and bottom bands of the shako in red, while they also wore red fringed epaulettes. Voltigeurs had side-chevrons and top and bottom bands of the shako in yellow, while their pompom was green and their plume was green tipped in yellow. In addition, they wore green epaulettes with yellow crescents and the collar of their jacket was yellow with dark blue piping. The Bardin Regulations tried to regularize the uniforms of the musicians by introducing a standard Imperial livery that was to be worn by all of them. This consisted of a dark green single-breasted jacket decorated with stripes of lace having alternate yellow and green segments. The yellow segments were decorated with an interwoven dark green crowned 'N', while the dark green segments were decorated with an interwoven yellow Imperial Eagle. Drum-majors were to have double silver lace on the collar, while ordinary musicians had the same decorative lace as the jacket on the collar and cuffs. Both collar and cuffs were red, whereas cuff flaps and shoulder straps were dark green and had red piping. Despite the new dress regulations, however, many bands continued to wear their previous regimental distinctions (such as busby hats or coloured trousers), of which they were particularly jealous.

During the brief restoration of the Bourbons in 1814, some elements of the line infantry uniforms were modified. For example, the tricolour cockade was replaced by the old white one, a new shako plate bearing the coat-of-arms of the royal family came into use and the 'N' badges were removed from the turnbacks of the fusiliers' jackets.

The standard equipment of the French line infantrymen remained the same during the period 1799–1815, consisting of the following basic elements: a knapsack made of calfskin tanned with hair on the outside that was carried on the back by means of buff leather shoulder straps, with a flap fastened by three buff leather straps and metal buckles; a black leather cartridge box constructed around a wooden block with holes for cartridges, which had an external flap over which a brass badge was applied (regimental number for fusiliers, flaming grenade for grenadiers and hunting horn for voltigeurs); a whitened buff leather crossbelt on which the cartridge box was suspended; and a whitened buff leather crossbelt to which the bayonet scabbard was suspended. The cartridge box was on the right hip, the bayonet scabbard on the left hip. The greatcoat was rolled on top of the knapsack and was kept in position by three white leather straps with metal buckles, while the fatigue cap was attached to the bottom part of the cartridge box. The bayonet scabbard was made of black leather and had brass fittings. Grenadiers and voltigeurs also carried a short sword, which was fastened together with the bayonet scabbard, and which scabbard was made of black leather with brass fittings. Non-regulation pieces of equipment that were often carried included canvas satchels of various dimensions and canteens. The latter ranged from wooden barrels to bottles with wicker-work cases, but metal flasks suspended on a coloured cord were also popular. On campaign, especially in the Iberian peninsula, dried pumpkins were often transformed into crude canteens. The standard weapon of the French line infantry was the M1777 Charleville musket, a smoothbore 17.5mm calibre flintlock with iron fittings that was 151.5cm long and weighed 4.375kg. Voltigeurs sometimes carried a shortened version of this weapon that was produced for the cavalry dragoons. The bayonet of the Charleville musket was 45.6cm long and triangular in section. Grenadiers and voltigeurs were also

Drummer of the line
infantry wearing the
1806 experimental
white uniform.

Drum-major of the line infantry with 1812 livery (left) and grenadier of the line infantry with winter campaign dress (right). Note the distinctive corded mace of the drum-major.

armed with an infantry *sabre-briquet*, or short sword, which had a cast-brass hilt and a curved guard ending in a pyramidal or rounded quillon. The blade of this weapon was curved like that of a cavalry sabre. The sword knot of the *sabre-briquet* was white for fusiliers, red for grenadiers and green with yellow tassel for voltigeurs. Officers carried a straight-bladed sword with single-bar guard and helmet-shaped pommel, which was suspended from a shoulder belt or a waistbelt passing beneath the front flap of the breeches. The scabbard of this elegant weapon was made of black leather and had gilded metal fittings. The sword knots of officers were golden.

Chapter 5

The Light Infantry, 1800–15

Organization

Broadly speaking, during the Napoleonic Period, the line and light regiments of the French infantry performed more or less the same tactical duties on the battlefield, since only the voltigeur companies of both the line and light units were true light infantrymen. The regiments of light infantry were more intensively trained in marksmanship than their line compatriots and were able to execute standard infantry manoeuvres with higher speed, but during large pitched battles they were mostly employed in line or column like the regiments of fusiliers. The chasseurs of the light regiments formed advance guards or scouting parties in front of the line units during marches, and this kind of service could be performed only by soldiers who were intelligent enough to judge the tactical situation independently from the orders received. As a result, in most cases the light infantry regiments had a superior military reputation compared with the line infantry. According to many contemporary observers, no light infantry corps in Europe was able to fight more effectively in open order than the French. More agile and better marksmen than the fusiliers, the chasseurs also proved quite effective when fighting in densely wooded areas or urban centres, where the line infantry usually experienced more difficulties in deploying. Physical fitness and boldness were key factors behind the success of the French light infantrymen, together with the flexibility of their units. Each company of chasseurs could be divided into three small sections when skirmishing. The left and right sections were tasked with firing upon the enemy from covert positions and had the bayonets removed from their muskets in order to be more agile, wheras the centre section was deployed in line, with bayonets fixed, to act as a screen behind which the other two sections could fall for protection in case of need. When skirmishing with the enemy, the French chasseurs' primary targets were officers and artillerymen: the former gave orders to the rank-and-file and thus played a critical role on the battlefield, while the latter were specialized troops and could not be easily replaced with standard infantry. In the Allied armies that fought against France, officers were more important than their French equivalents, since Allied soldiers were largely unable to act independently without orders from

Drummers of the light infantry with 1801 shako.

their officers like the French did. As a result, killing the officers of an enemy unit meant paralyzing it on the battlefield. Firing at enemy artillerymen also had a great tactical advantage, since killing gunners was much easier than capturing or destroying enemy guns by frontal charge as it could be done from a distance and without losing soldiers.

It should be remembered, however, that French chasseurs were all armed with the same standard muskets as the line infantry, and these heavy smoothbores had poor rates of accuracy from long distance. The excellent performances of Napoleon's light

Musicians of a light infantry regiment. Note the coloured bands of lace worn on the sleeves.

infantrymen were thus more the result of their great determination and good training than of the quality of their equipment. In several Allied armies, the light infantry were equipped with rifled carbines and therefore had a significant technological advantage over the French light regiments. It should be remembered, however, that no other military power in Europe had so many light infantry units as France. As in the pre-1789 years, French chasseurs continued to be mostly recruited from mountainous departments throughout the Napoleonic Period. The emperor knew that the communities living in the French mountains contained a high percentage of hunters, trained to be excellent marksmen since their childhood, who were used to moving very rapidly on broken terrain. As a result, volunteers and recruits from the departments of the Alps and the Pyrenees were usually assigned to the light infantry regiments rather than the line ones. Napoleon always paid great attention to the training of his light infantry corps, but on several occasions was forced to 'forget' the peculiarities of his chasseurs and employ them as standard line infantry. Nevertheless, even when deployed in line or column, the French light infantrymen still showed all their valour and courage.

In 1799, according to the general reorganization that had taken place in 1795 and 1796, the French infantry comprised a total of thirty light demi-brigades, numbered from 1–30. Each of these half-brigades consisted of three battalions, which by now had a quite homogenous composition in terms of training and experience. A single battalion consisted of one carabinier company and nine chasseur companies. It should be remembered, however, that chasseurs of the light units corresponded to fusiliers of the line formations, and that carabiniers of the light units corresponded to grenadiers of the line ones. A single company consisted of the following elements: one captain, one lieutenant, one sub-lieutenant, one sergeant-major, five sergeants, one corporal-fourrier, eight corporals, two horn players and 104 privates. The elite carabinier companies had a similar structure, but with four sergeants and sixty-four privates. The staff of each half-brigade comprised one colonel, three battalion commanders, one adjutant, one paymaster, one drum-major, three standard-bearers, one surgeon, four assistant surgeons, one shoemaker, one gaiter maker, one gunsmith, one tailor and eight musicians. On 24 September 1803, Napoleon's decision to replace the term demi-brigade with the regiment also applied to the light infantry. The amalgamation of the regulars with the volunteers had been completed several years before, and thus there was no point in using this old denomination that was too 'revolutionary' for the First Consul's tastes. The passage from half-brigade to regiment did not affect the numbering of the units and did not introduce any modification of their internal structure. During 1803, however, Napoleon was obliged to intervene in the general structure of his light infantry, since several regiments had to be disbanded following the French defeat in Haiti. After becoming First Consul, Napoleon did his best to restore order in the Caribbean colony and, as we have seen, sent a large expeditionary force to Haiti. This expedition, comprising several demi-brigades of light infantry, was practically destroyed by yellow fever and the rebellious slaves. Following the defeat in Haiti, Napoleon had to disband four of his light infantry regiments – the 11th, 19th, 20th and 30th – which remained vacant from that time. Due to this reduction, the French light infantry comprised twenty-six regiments in December 1803, although a new 31st Light Regiment was created in 1804 from the remnants of the four units that had been disbanded during the previous year.

In 1804, Napoleon introduced voltigeurs into his light infantry battalions in order to have some specialized skirmishers in the chasseur regiments. Instead of adding more soldiers to each battalion and in order to retain the standard number of ten companies for each unit, Napoleon ordered that the second company of chasseurs in each light infantry battalion should retrain in order to become a voltigeur company. These became an elite sub-unit like the carabinier company that was already in each battalion. As a result, from 1804, each light infantry battalion started to have two elite companies and eight chasseur companies. The voltigeur companies then started to be detached – quite frequently – from their parent battalions in order to form temporary ad hoc battalions of elite skirmishers. These were employed to conduct special operations, including storming enemy positions or conducting long-range scouting missions. When a light infantry battalion was deployed in line on the battlefield, the carabinier company was placed on the right and the voltigeur company on the left. Consequently, as was the case with the line infantry, the two elite companies were also known as flank companies to differentiate them from the centre companies of chasseurs. Generally speaking, the carabiniers were selected from the tallest and strongest recruits assigned to each battalion, whereas the voltigeurs were chosen from the smallest since they had to move quickly around the battlefield. Both carabiniers and voltigeurs usually had some combat experience, being chosen from veterans who had already served for several years. After 1804, the general structure of the French light infantry saw no significant changes until 1808: these were the years of Napoleon's greatest victories and of the proclamation of the French Empire. The French light infantrymen showed their valour in a series of memorable pitched battles at Ulm, Austerlitz, Jena, Auerstadt, Eylau and Friedland. The French chasseurs were well disciplined and could adapt to any tactical situation, being similarly able to launch frontal bayonet assaults or skirmish on any kind of terrain.

On 18 February 1808, Napoleon modified the organization of his light infantry as he did the line formations by enlarging it significantly but without creating any new regiments. According to the new reforms, each light infantry regiment was to consist of four active battalions – known as *bataillons de guerre* – plus one depot battalion, which was smaller than the others since it consisted of just four chasseur companies. Each *bataillon de guerre* comprised one company of carabiniers, one company of voltigeurs and four companies of chasseurs. As a result, a light infantry regiment now had four companies of carabiniers, four companies of voltigeurs, sixteen companies of chasseurs and four depot companies. The depot companies were mostly tasked with providing new recruits to the *bataillons de guerre* as replacements. The staff of each regiment now consisted of one colonel, one major,

Horn player of a light infantry regiment (voltigeur company) wearing 1812 livery. Note the brown campaign trousers.

Light infantryman of the
Volontaires Bonaparte.

Soldiers of the Garde Municipale de Paris: 1st Regiment
(left) and 2nd Regiment (right).

four battalion commanders, five adjutants, five assistants, ten sergeant-majors, one drum-major, one drum-corporal, one bandmaster, seven musicians, four craftsmen, one quartermaster, one paymaster, one surgeon-major and four assistant surgeons. Unlike the line regiments, the light regiments did not have the three standard-bearers, since Napoleon did not assign an Imperial Eagle to each light infantry regiment but just one battalion standard to each of the four active battalions that made up a chasseur regiment. The emperor wanted the battalions of the light regiments to serve as detached and independent units on most occasions, so there was no point in assigning a single Imperial Eagle to the whole regiment. The commander of each light battalion chose one veteran NCO from the companies under his command who would carry the battalion standard.

A single light infantry company now comprised one captain, one lieutenant, one sub-lieutenant, one sergeant-major, four sergeants, one corporal-quartermaster, eight corporals, two horn players and 121 privates. The carabinier and voltigeur companies had the same standard internal establishment. Carabiniers were chosen from soldiers who already had four years of service and had fought in at least two of the following battles: Ulm, Austerlitz, Jena and Friedland. A carabinier had to be at least 173.5cm tall. Voltigeurs, meanwhile, were selected from troops with at least two years of service, and had to be under 150cm tall. Both the carabiniers and voltigeurs received higher pay than the chasseurs due to their elite status.

As was the case with the line units, the depot battalion of a light regiment was commanded by a major and did not go off to war. There was a different function for each of its four companies. The main task of the 4th Company, which did not leave the depot, was to dress and train the new recruits, so the unit had a dressing captain and a quartermaster-treasurer. The 1st and 3rd Company, meanwhile, transferred the newly trained recruits to their battalions, while the 2nd Company tended to act as a garrison duties in the various military facilities. Sons or orphans of soldiers on the battalion's payroll – known as the *enfants de troupe* – were attached to the 4th Company, as were veteran soldiers awaiting retirement or their pension.

The four *bataillons de guerre* of each regiment included four sapeurs (pioneers) each, who were attached to the carabinier company and were placed under the command of a pioneer corporal (there was one such NCO for each regiment). The sappers acted as combat engineers, constructing field fortifications and removing any obstacle that was encountered by the battalion during their march. They had the same status and privileges as the carabiniers.

The internal organization of the French light infantry units introduced in 1808 remained practically unchanged until the end of the Napoleonic Period in 1815. Between 1805 and 1815, however, the general establishment of the French light troops was increased with the formation of new units. The first of these to be created was the 32nd Light Regiment, which was formed in 1805 by assembling together the two infantry battalions of the army of the Ligurian Republic. A puppet state of France since 1797, the Ligurian Republic was annexed to the empire in 1805 and its small military forces were absorbed into the French Army. The two Ligurian battalions, despite being line units, already had a distinct light infantry character before becoming part of the French light troops.

In 1810, the Kingdom of Holland, which was ruled by Napoleon's younger brother, Louis Bonaparte, as a puppet state of France from 1806, was annexed to the French Empire, with its armed forces absorbed into the French Army. Thanks to the incorporation of the Dutch infantry units, the French light infantry could raise the new 33rd Light Regiment. A unit bearing this denomination had already existed in 1808 and 1809, but it had been a temporary formation that was soon disbanded after having been created for service in the Iberian peninsula. In 1809, Napoleon, in order to create more infantry units to fight in Spain, had formed seven temporary auxiliary battalions by bringing together different detachments of line infantry regiments that were already serving in the Iberian peninsula. In 1811, these battalions were assembled together to form two new regular regiments (one of line infantry and one of light infantry). The 1st, 3rd and 6th Auxiliary Battalions became the 130th Line Regiment, while the 2nd, 4th, 5th and 7th Auxiliary Battalions became the 34th Light Regiment. That same year, Napoleon decided to re-raise the 11th Light Regiment that had been disbanded in 1803, following the defeat in Haiti, by gathering together four special/foreign battalions that ceased to be independent corps during that year (which will be covered more fully in a following chapter): the Tirailleurs Corses (from Corsica), the Tirailleurs du Po (from the former Duchy of Parma), the Tirailleurs de la Légion du Midi (from Piedmont) and the Valaisan Battalion (from Switzerland). Despite its very composite nature, the new 11th Light Regiment proved to be an effective unit. On 8 June 1808, following the annexation of Tuscany to the empire, Napoleon ordered the creation of a new battalion made up of conscripts from the new Italian departments who had so far avoided conscription. This semi-penal unit had a light infantry character from its foundation and became a regiment in 1810 (with five battalions). Its official denomination was the 1st Mediterranean Regiment. In March 1811, a 2nd Mediterranean Regiment of the same nature was formed, but this was soon absorbed into the French line units as the 133rd Regiment. In 1812, the 1st Mediterranean Regiment was also absorbed into the French infantry as the 35th Light Regiment.

In 1812, a new 36th Light Regiment was added to the general structure of the chasseur units; this had a very peculiar history that started some years before.

Soldiers of the Garde Municipale de Paris: fusilier of the 1st Regiment (left) and grenadier of the 2nd Regiment (right).

Voltigeur of the
2nd Regiment
of the Garde
Municipale de
Paris. Curiously,
he is wearing a
bearskin instead
of the shako.

Following Britain's blockade of continental Europe's ports, Napoleon decided to organize some locally raised infantry battalions that could protect his empire's most exposed tracts of coastline. He in particular wanted to defend the small French islands that could be attacked and seized by the Royal Navy. Consequently, in 1810, three such battalions were formed on three small islands that had a major military importance: the Battalion of Belle Ile, the Battalion of Ile de Ré and the Battalion of Walcheren. Belle Ile is located on the southern coast of Brittany, while Ile de Ré is off La Rochelle in Aquitaine and Walcheren is on the coast of Zealand (in the Netherlands, which had been annexed by France). All three islands were extremely important from a naval point of view, and their capture by the British had to be avoided at all costs. A British expeditionary corps had occupied Walcheren for several weeks in 1809, and Napoleon had learned from this experience. In 1811, the Battalion of Belle Ile was transformed into a five-battalion regiment by absorbing some Italian conscripts who had initially been assigned to the 2nd Mediterranean Regiment. In 1812, due to its good conduct, the Regiment of Belle Ile was absorbed into the French infantry as the 36th Light Regiment. On 7 February 1812, some weeks before the beginning of Napoleon's ill-fated Russian campaign, the new 37th Light Regiment was created from several detachments that were provided by the garrison battalions of the existing chasseur regiments. In December 1813, Napoleon re-raised the 19th Light Regiment that had been disbanded in 1803 following the French defeat in Haiti. The new unit was formed from the survivors of several battalions that had returned from the Russian campaign: the 4th Battalion of the 1st Light Regiment, the 3rd Battalion of the 3rd Light Regiment, the 1st Battalion and 2nd Battalion of the 22nd Light Regiment and the 1st Battalion of the 35th Light Regiment. Following the first abdication of Napoleon, the restored French monarchy significantly reduced the number of light infantry regiments of the French Army on 12 May 1814, with the chasseur units reduced to just fifteen (numbered from 1–15). When Napoleon returned to France from his exile on Elba in 1815, he did not change the new structure of 15 light infantry regiments, but restored the old numeration. Generally speaking, the reduction ordered by the restored monarchy in 1814 had some positive effects, since by licensing the most inexperienced regiments, the remaining fifteen could fill their ranks with the best elements of the disbanded units.

Uniforms and equipment

In 1799, French light infantrymen were still dressed in the national uniform that had been introduced in 1793. This was similar to that worn by the line infantry, but was medium blue instead of dark blue and had some elements in medium blue rather than in white (such as the frontal lapels of the coat, the waistcoat and trousers). The standard uniform of a chasseur in 1799 was as follows: black bicorn with tricolour national cockade and half-green and half-red woollen tuft, medium blue short-tailed coat with red collar and round cuffs piped in white, medium blue frontal lapels piped in white, medium blue shoulder straps piped in white, medium blue turnbacks piped in white, red cuff flaps piped in white, medium blue vertical pocket flaps on the back of the coat piped in white and having three buttons, brass buttons, medium blue waistcoat, medium blue trousers and black half-boots with white piping on the top and white tassel on the front. Carabiniers wore the same dress but with the distinctive elements used by the line infantry's grenadiers: red fringed epaulettes instead of the standard shoulder straps and black bearskin cap with tricolour cockade, red cords and flounders, red plume and red crown with a white cross. Differently from that of the grenadiers, the bearskin of the carabiniers did not have a brass frontal plate. The cuffs of the coat could be pointed in some cases, and the cuff-flaps worn by officers and NCOs could sometimes have a different shape, which were the most common non-regulation features to be found on light infantry uniforms. These variations derived from the fact that uniforms were produced on a local basis, but over time they became much rarer as Napoleon strove to dress his soldiers alike. Other non-regulation modifications included the lack of white piping to the frontal lapels and the use of horizontal pocket flaps on the back of the coat (instead of the vertical ones prescribed by regulations). On the turnbacks, like for the line infantry, there were embroidered company badges: white hunting horns for chasseurs and red flaming grenades for carabiniers. Most of the regiments eventually substituted their original brass buttons with white metal ones, which bore a hunting horn and the regimental number. The waistcoat had to be single-breasted according to official regulations, but it was not uncommon to find it in a double-breasted version; it had to be medium blue, but red and white ones were also quite popular. Sometimes, especially after 1800, the normal shoulder straps of the chasseurs could be replaced with non-regulation green epaulettes with or without red crescents. The top piping and frontal tassel of the half-boots had to be white for chasseurs and red for carabiniers, although it was not uncommon to find them in green. A handful of the features of the uniform described were later slightly modified: the tails of the coat became shorter in order to be more practical, for example, and the frontal lapels started to have an accentuated curve. According to official regulations, the trousers of the light infantry had to be medium blue during summer, but white trousers were also quite popular during the warmer months.

Carabinier of the Chasseurs de Montagne.

Carabinier of the
Tirailleurs Corses in
1815. Note the two
pistols worn at the
waist.

On 26 October 1801, the light infantry regiments' black bicorn was replaced by the shako. It should be noted, however, that some chasseur units had already been wearing non-regulation shakos well before 1801. These were of the mirliton type, which imitated contemporary light cavalry fashions and consisted of a cloth 'wing' that was wrapped around the body of a tall peakless cap. The tall cap was black and the cloth 'wing' was usually green or yellow. On the left side of the cap there could be a half-yellow and half-green plume in addition to the national cockade, while the 'wing' could have a green or yellow tassel at its end. The shako introduced by the 1801 dress regulations was the direct heir of this non-regulation mirliton headgear, but it did not have the cloth 'wing' that characterized the latter. It was quite squat but widened slightly towards the top. On the front it had a detachable peak that was set not on the very lower edge of the headgear, but a short way up the body of the cap. The peak was fastened by hooks and eyes. The shako was constructed of black felt, with black leather top and bottom bands. It was ornamented on the front with a brass badge of a hunting-horn shape, while on the left side of the headgear there was the national cockade secured by an orange-yellow lace holder. Wrapped around the headgear there were green decorative cords and flounders, and on the left side of the shako there was a drooping plume in green for chasseurs and red for carabiniers. The top and bottom bands of the carabiniers' shakos were red instead of black, and they additionally had red cords and flounders and a different brass badge on the front (bearing a flaming grenade). With the introduction of the shako, the bearskins of the carabiniers started to be worn only for parade or for combat, becoming much rarer to see. Sometimes the plume and cockade of the shako could be fixed on the front rather than the left side, since the peak of the headgear could be detached.

When the voltigeurs were introduced into the French Army in 1804, they received a distinctive uniform that included a yellow collar piped in white and green epaulettes with or without a red crescent. They wore a black shako with brass frontal plate, yellow cords and flounders, black top and bottom bands, black peak, national cockade, and half-yellow and half-green plume; medium blue short-tailed coat with yellow collar piped in white, medium blue round cuffs piped in white, medium blue frontal lapels piped in white, green epaulettes with red crescent, medium blue turnbacks piped in white and having yellow hunting horn badges, red cuff flaps piped in white, medium blue vertical pocket flaps on the back of the coat piped in white and having three buttons, white metal buttons; medium blue waistcoat; medium blue trousers; and black half-boots with yellow piping on the top and yellow tassel on the front. Some non-regulation variations of this dress existed: the yellow collar could be piped in red, while the cuff flaps could be yellow instead of red and the cuffs could be pointed rather than rounded. The piping and tassel of the half-boots could be white or green in alternative to yellow. Furthermore, the cords and flounders of the shako could be white or green in alternative to yellow. Between 1804 and 1806, several companies of voltigeurs replaced their shakos with non-regulation busby hats made of brown or black fur, which were copied from those worn by the light cavalry. These had yellow 'bags' of cloth on the back and a half-yellow and half-green plume. Sometimes they were also worn by the carabinier companies, with a red 'bag' of cloth on the back and red plume. All the light infantrymen wore loose trousers during most of their daily life and tighter-fitting breeches on campaign or on parade. While in their barracks, the NCOs and rankers usually wore only their medium blue waistcoats, which were long-sleeved and single-breasted. These could sometimes have red collar and round cuffs, details that were not prescribed in the official regulations. The waistcoat had two horizontal pocket flaps on the front and two white metal buttons on each cuff; when wearing it on campaign, grenadiers and voltigeurs added their distinctive epaulettes to the waistcoat. Until 1805, for winter use, both the line and light infantrymen did not receive greatcoats produced for the Army, and thus had to wear their own civilian overcoats or cloaks. In 1805 and 1806, greatcoats were issued to most of the regiments for the first time. These were usually single-breasted, but could also be double-breasted. Their colour was not standardized, but they tended to be beige, brown or grey. The greatcoats of officers were usually dark blue. The light infantrymen also used the *bonnet de police* as an undress cap, which was medium blue with white piping and had a tasselled stocking end folded up and tucked behind the right-hand side of a stiffened headband. The tassel was white, and on the front of the cap there was a red flaming grenade for carabinier companies.

According to the egalitarian principles of the Revolution, officers were dressed exactly like their men, but their uniforms were of finer material. In addition, compared with those of NCOs and rankers, their uniforms had longer tails. The shakos of the officers had silver frontal plates and silver cords and flounders; their top band was decorated in the form of silver laurel leaves or silver interlocking rings embroidered on a black velvet backing. Officers wore a gilt gorget under their neck, which was mostly used on parade and incorporated decorative silver devices that usually included unit number and – after 1804 – an Imperial Eagle. Officers showed their rank on their uniforms with silver lace epaulettes that were worn on the shoulders; these were designed according to the same general scheme that was used by the line infantry. Each rank corresponded to a different combination of the epaulettes: colonels had epaulettes with bullion fringes on both shoulders; majors had epaulettes with bullion fringes and silver straps; battalion commanders had bullion fringes only on the left epaulette; captains had gold lace fringes only on the left epaulette; adjutants had gold lace fringes only on the right epaulette; lieutenants had them like captains, but with one red stripe on the straps; sub-lieutenants had them like captains, but with two red stripes on the straps; and adjutant-NCOs had red straps with two golden stripes and mixed red-and-gold fringes only on the left epaulette. While on active service, the officers frequently replaced their coat with a single-breasted tunic without lapels known as a *surtout*, or overall; this was entirely medium blue, with white piping to the collar, front and round cuffs. Like the coat, however, it had the epaulettes showing rank on the shoulders. NCOs' ranks were shown by diagonal bars of lace that were applied on the lower sleeves, while there were two white bars for corporals, one silver bar piped in red for sergeants and two silver bars piped in red for sergeant-majors. Both NCOs and rankers had lace service chevrons on the upper sleeves of their coats; these were worn point uppermost and were silver for senior NCOs or red for junior NCOs and other ranks. The number of chevrons corresponded to the years of service: one for ten years of service, two for fifteen years and three for twenty years. The same epaulettes, rank bars and service chevrons worn on the coat were also applied on the greatcoat.

Carabinier of the Tirailleurs Corses in 1815. Note the peculiar Corsican ventral pouch.

Grenadier (left) and voltigeur (right) of the 3rd Swiss Regiment. Note the peculiar brass plate of the bearskin.

In February 1806 there was a notable modification in the uniforms of the French infantry, with a new model of shako introduced for both the line and the light regiments. The new headgear had a body made of black felt or board, which widened slightly towards the top, and a waterproofed crown. Around the top and bottom of the shako there were leather bands that reinforced it, and on the front there was a leather peak. A leather chevron was usually applied for strengthening on each side of the shako. On the front of the top band was a tricolour cockade placed above a lozenge-shaped brass plate that bore an embossed Imperial Eagle and the number of the regiment. The shako was held in place by brass chinscales that comprised circular bosses, the first of which on each side, on the bottom band of the headgear, was larger than the others and had a decorative badge (a hunting horn for chasseurs and voltigeurs or a flaming grenade for carabiniers). Above the cockade was a woollen pompom for chasseurs and a plume for carabiniers and voltigeurs. The pompom was in company colour, while the plume of carabiniers was red and that of voltigeurs was yellow with a green tip. Wrapped around the shako were decorative cords and flounders, which were usually removed while on campaign – these were white for chasseurs, red for carabiniers and green for voltigeurs. The shakos of the officers had silver lace on the top band, silver cords and flounders, silver lace holder for the cockade and gilded fittings. With the introduction of the new shako in 1806, the bearskin of the carabiniers was officially done away with, although it was still worn by some companies for a number of years. The sSapeurs continued to be dressed like the carabiniers for the whole period taken into account here, but with a few distinctions: for example, they had a distinctive badge, consisting of two crossed axes, embroidered in red or white on the sleeves. The sappers also retained their bearskin after 1806, which could be replaced by a smaller busby hat. They carried several special pieces of equipment, such as white leather gauntlets, white leather apron and white leather axe-case. Beards were mandatory for sappers and were extremely popular too among carabiniers. Except for one unit (the 4th Light Regiment), the light infantry units were not affected by the introduction of the 1806 experimental white uniform.

The medium blue uniforms of the French light infantry remained unchanged until 9 November 1810, when a new model of shako was introduced. This was slightly taller and more robust than the previous one; it did not have chevrons on the sides and did not have cords or flounders. The latter, however, continued to be worn by most of the regiments. The new shako was intended to have a pompom for carabiniers and voltigeurs instead of the plume, but this feature was never adopted: the carabiniers simply added a red pompom to the base of their red plumes and the voltigeurs a yellow pompom at the base of their yellow plumes tipped in green. The frontal plate of the new shako was lozenge-shaped and bore the distinctive number of each regiment inside a hunting horn for chasseurs/voltigeurs and a flaming grenade for carabiniers. Several units, however, used a different kind of brass plate that was crescent-shaped and bore an Imperial Eagle. This alternative design, which was not prescribed by official regulations, became so popular that it was officially adopted with the new dress regulations of 1812. In February 1811, the system of pompoms and plumes for the headgear was regularized as follows: colonels had to wear an entirely white plume, majors a white-over-red plume and battalion commanders an entirely red plume; all other officers and the NCOs of the regimental staff were to have white pompoms. Carabiniers would have a red pompom, voltigeurs a yellow one. Each of the four chasseur companies in a light infantry battalion wore pompoms in a different colour, but unlike what happened for the line infantry, these four colours varied for each regiment. Sometimes the pompom could bear the battalion number in white and could be surmounted by a tuft in the same colour, but these variations were not permitted according to official dress regulations. On the new shako introduced during 1810, the silver top band worn by officers had a different width according to rank. Shako covers were used by most of the soldiers, in order to protect their precious headgear on campaign; these were made of black waterproof fabric or of buff cotton. The covers concealed most of the shako's decorations, except for the pompom/plume. Sometimes regimental numbers or regimental badges could be painted on the front of these covers. On campaign, loose trousers or overalls were extremely common; they could be grey, ochre, brown or medium blue according to the clothing materials that were available locally. During long marches, the trousers were turned up at the bottom or were tied around the ankle with string, while the greatcoat was frequently worn directly over the waistcoat and the medium blue coat was carried in the knapsack.

The uniforms of the light infantry musicians were governed, until the 1812 dress regulations, by the personal tastes of the colonels commanding each regiment. The members of the regimental band wore coats in extravagant colours, such as yellow or green, and frequently hadh non-regulation headgear, for example bicorns with ostrich-feathers or *czapkas*. The uniforms of the regimental bandsmen were very colourful. Their facings were all trimmed with multi-coloured lace, they had trefoil-shaped epaulettes in the same colour as the trimming and sometimes also decorative shoulder wings worn under the epaulettes. Trousers could be decorated on the front with embroidered knots, while the regulation footwear was usually replaced with black leather half-boots with coloured top edging and front tassel. Plumes, pompoms, cords and flounders on shakos could be in various colours (which usually matched that of the coat or the trimming). Drum-majors had the

Grenadier of the 3rd Swiss Regiment with 1812 dress.

most ornate uniforms, including a black bicorn trimmed with silver lace and large plumes (usually in the national colours of France – red, white and blue). They also had leather gauntlets and a laced baldric made of cloth to support their ornamental sabre, but their most important mark of distinction was the corded mace with which they directed the regimental band. In most cases, the trimming of the drum-majors' uniforms was silver, to match the epaulettes that they wore on the shoulders.

Fusilier officers (left) and voltigeur officer (right) of the 3rd Swiss Regiment.

Instead of the bicorn, the drum-majors could have a busby made of fur that was similar to that of the French light cavalry. Drum-corporals were dressed similarly to drum-majors, but had fewer decorations. The musicians of each company were dressed in a much simpler way, and looked very similar to the regular foot soldiers. They had coloured lacing on the facings, pockets and turnbacks, and usually had decorative stripes of coloured lace on the sleeves and coloured shoulder-wings.

Shako ornaments, company distinctions, badges on the turnbacks and epaulettes were all the same as the ordinary soldiers.

On 19 January 1812, new dress regulations were brought in for the French infantry, named after the officer responsible for their issue, Major Bardin. The new uniform for the light infantry, like that of their line infantry comrades, was similar to the previous one but had some modifications. The old light infantry coat was replaced with a double-breasted and short-tailed medium blue jacket, the *habit-veste*, with plastron-style lapels on the front and vertical pockets on the back. The medium blue short turnbacks had a white hunting horn for chasseurs, a red flaming grenade for carabiniers and a yellow hunting horn for voltigeurs. Chasseurs had medium blue shoulder straps piped in white, while voltigeurs had yellow shoulder straps piped in medium blue and carabiniers red shoulder straps piped in medium blue. Rank distinctions and service chevrons remained the same. The medium blue waistcoat, no longer visible under the jacket, now had a lower collar and the same shoulder straps as the coat. Black or white gaiters no longer extended over the knee. The 1812 regulations also introduced a new model of shako, with a white metal frontal plate that had a crowned Imperial Eagle on a semi-circular plate into which the regimental number was cut inside a hunting horn. The tricolour cockade and white metal chinscales of the old model of shako were retained, and although cords and flounders were officially abolished, in practice they were still worn by the majority of regiments. Carabiniers' shakos had red top and bottom bands as well as red side-chevrons, whereas those of the voltigeurs had yellow top and bottom bands and yellow side-chevrons. The shakos of the chasseurs had tufted pompoms in company colour (green for the 1st Company, sky blue for the 2nd Company, orange for the 3rd Company and violet for the 4th Company), while those of the elite companies had a tufted pompom and plume in red for carabiniers and yellow for voltigeurs. The light infantry also had the new model of pie-shaped forage cap known as the pokalem, the same as the line infantry but in medium blue. The light infantry pokalem was piped in white and bore the regimental number or the grenadier or voltigeur badge embroidered in white on the front.

Under the new 1812 dress regulations, the uniform of a chasseur was now as follows: black shako with black top and bottom bands, white metal chinscales and frontal plate, and national cockade and pompom in company colour; medium blue *habit-veste* with medium blue collar and pointed cuffs piped in white, medium blue shoulder straps piped in white, medium blue frontal plastron piped in white, white metal buttons, medium blue short turnbacks piped in white with embroidered company badge, and medium blue vertical pocket flaps piped in white on the back of the jacket; medium blue trousers, and black or white gaiters. Carabiniers had a plume, pompom, side-chevrons, and top and bottom bands of the shako in red, while voltigeurs had them in yellow. In addition, the collar of their jacket was yellow with white piping. Despite what was prescribed in the new regulations, almost all the carabinier and voltigeur companies continued to wear their coloured epaulettes after 1812.

The Bardin Regulations attempted to regularize the uniforms of the musicians with a standard Imperial livery worn by all of them. For musicians in light infantry units, this was the same as those described previously for the line infantry, but their dark green single-breasted jacket had collar, cuffs and shoulder straps in green. However, despite the new dress regulations, many regimental bands jealously continued to wear parts of their previous uniform, such as busby hats.

During the brief restoration of the Bourbons under Louis XVIII in 1814, some elements of the light infantry uniforms were modified, with the tricolour cockade replaced by the old white one and a new shako plate bearing the coat-of-arms of the royal family coming into use.

The standard equipment of the French light infantrymen remained the same between 1799 and 1815, consisting of the following basic elements: a knapsack made of calfskin tanned with hair on the outside, carried on the back by means of buff leather shoulder straps, with a flap fastened by three buff leather straps and metal buckles; a black leather cartridge box constructed around a wooden block, with holes for cartridges and an external flap over which a white metal badge was applied (flaming grenade for carabiniers and hunting horn for chasseurs/voltigeurs); a whitened buff leather crossbelt to which the cartridge box was suspended; and a whitened buff leather crossbelt to which the bayonet scabbard was suspended. The cartridge box was on the right hip, and the bayonet scabbard on the left hip. The greatcoat was carried on top of the knapsack and was kept in position with three white leather straps with metal buckles. The fatigue cap was attached to the bottom part of the cartridge box. The bayonet scabbard was made of black leather and had brass fittings. Differently from the line infantry, all the companies of a light infantry battalion carried a short sword that was fastened to the bayonet scabbard. The short sword had a scabbard made of black leather with brass fittings. Non-regulation pieces of equipment that were often carried included canvas satchels of various dimensions and canteens. The latter ranged from wooden barrels to bottles in wicker cases, as well as metal flasks suspended on a coloured cord. On campaign, particularly in Spain and Portugal, dried pumpkins were often made into rudimentary canteens. The standard weapon of the French chasseurs, like that of the line infantry, was the smoothbore 17.5mm M1777 Charleville musket. This was produced in a shortened 141.7cm long version specifically designed for light infantry, weighing 4.375kg. The bayonet of the Charleville musket was 45.6cm long and triangular in section. The

Sapper of the 3rd Swiss
Regiment. Note the long
beard and the peculiar badges
embroidered on the sleeves.

Officer and soldiers of the Valais Battalion.

sabre-briquet, or short sword, had a cast-brass hilt and a curved guard ending in a pyramidal or rounded quillon. The blade of this weapon was curved like that of a cavalry sabre. The sword knot of the *sabre-briquet* was green for chasseurs, red for carabiniers and yellow for voltigeurs. Just as in the line infantry, light infantry officers carried a straight-bladed sword with single-bar guard and helmet-shaped pommel, suspended from a shoulder belt or a waistbelt passing beneath the front flap of the breeches. The scabbard was made of black leather and had gilded metal fittings, and the sword knots were silver.

Chapter 6

Special Infantry Units

The French infantry comprised a number of special units that did not belong to the general structure of the line infantry or the light infantry. These performed specific duties, but had much in common with the line or light regiments in terms of training and uniforms.

Volontaires Bonaparte: After returning from his Egyptian campaign, during the latter months of 1799 Napoleon found his Army of Italy in a deplorable situation. The Austro-Russians had obtained a series of victories during his absence and practically all the territorial gains that France had achieved in 1796 and 1797 had been lost. The Army of Italy had to be rebuilt almost from scratch, since it had been all but destroyed as an effective force in a series of reverses. In order to attract more volunteers and to have a corps of loyal supporters who would follow him on the battlefields of northern Italy and the Rhineland, Napoleon authorized the creation of new volunteer corps on 8 March 1800 that would be formed by enthusiastic youngsters from the middle classes of the Republic. Three such new units were soon formed, receiving the denomination of Bonaparte's Volunteers, although they were also known as the First Consul's Reserve Legion. Of the three units, two were battalions of light infantry and one a regiment of hussars. Most of the young men who joined the ranks of Bonaparte's Volunteers wanted to serve as cavalrymen, but they could not provide themselves with horses and thus had to act as light infantrymen. However, the government, to boost their morale, provided them with elegant uniforms. Each of the two battalions of light infantry had nine companies, which were later grouped together to form a temporary demi-brigade, while the hussar regiment continued to act independently. In the early weeks of 1801, after having seen little action, Bonaparte's Volunteers were disbanded and their members were absorbed into various regular units (those of the 1st Battalion were included in the 45th line half-brigade, and those of the 2nd Battalion in the 17th light half-brigade). The light infantry uniform of this corps was very elegant, comprising a black Corsican hat and a light blue coat. The coat had its collar, pointed cuffs, frontal lapels, shoulder straps and turnbacks in yellow. The Corsican hat was adorned with a national cockade and a light blue plume on the brim, that

Uniforms of the Neuchatel Battalion (from left to right): voltigeur, officer and grenadier.

Uniforms of the Neuchatel Battalion (from left to right): voltigeur, officer and sapper.

was turned up on the left side. The hat was also surmounted by a black crest, and around it was a wrapped band of light blue cloth. The uniform was completed by white double-breasted waistcoat and trousers, worn with black half-boots that had top piping and a frontal tassel in white.

Garde Municipale de Paris: The capital of France had always had a special guard corps acting both as the garrison of the city and as a sort of urban police that was tasked with keeping order in the metropolis. In 1789, the Paris Guard sided with the revolutionaries, and was consequently retained in service by the new government. Two years later, however, it was disbanded following the general reorganization of the Gendarmerie (France's militarized police). With the creation and expansion of the National Guard, which counted on several units in Paris, for several years the French capital did not have an independent corps of military police. This situation came to an end in 1802, when First Consul Napoleon decided to create a strong corps of militarized policemen who could keep order in his capital; Paris, especially until the proclamation of the Empire, was always on the verge of revolt and its popular masses were a potential menace for any ruling government. In addition, the French capital was the main base of all the royalist and foreign spies who were active in France. The new Municipal Guard of Paris came into existence on 4 October 1802, consisting of two half-brigades (regiments after 1804) that were mostly recruited from old veterans of the French Army as well as former members of the Gendarmerie. These men were experienced soldiers and policemen, since each of them had to have served for at least ten years and to have participated in at least five military campaigns. The 1st half-brigade was tasked with guarding all the entrances to the French capital, while the 2nd garrisoned various areas of the vast city. Attached to the two infantry units was a squadron of dragoons, which patrolled the major streets and acted as an 'honour guard' when needed.

Until 18 May 1806, the Municipal Guard of Paris was under control of the city's civilian authorities, but from that date it was transferred to the authority of the Ministry of War. The two infantry demi-brigades consisted of two battalions with five companies each, while the squadron of dragoons had just two mounted companies. From 1805, the first battalion of each half-brigade was sent to serve with the regular armed forces, and participated in military campaigns from 1805–07 as part of the French Army's reserves. Between 1808 and 1812, the composite demi-brigade of the Municipal Guard serving with the army fought with great distinction in Spain, where its members highlighted their valour as veteran soldiers. On 12 February 1812, the units that were stationed in Paris were reorganized as a single regiment of line infantry with two battalions, each of which had one company of grenadiers, one company of voltigeurs and four companies of fusiliers. On 23 October 1812, while Napoleon was in Russia, the Municipal Guard of Paris participated in a failed military coup that was organized against the emperor by General Malet. This marked the end of the corps, with Napoleon reacting to the coup by returning to Paris and disbanding the Municipal Guard. Its members, as mentioned in a previous chapter, were absorbed into the 134th Line Regiment. The squadron of dragoons, which had not taken part in the failed coup, was absorbed into the Dutch Lancers of the Imperial Guard in February 1813.

The two infantry regiments of the Municipal Guard of Paris were dressed in colourful uniforms, leading to its members commonly being known as the *perroquets*, or 'little parrots'. The 1st Regiment had a dark green uniform with red facings, while the 2nd Regiment had a red uniform with dark green facings. All the general features of the uniform were the same as that worn by the line infantry. In 1806, when several line regiments received the experimental white uniform as described in one of the previous chapters, the Municipal Guard of Paris was also dressed in white. Their new uniform was like that introduced for the line regiments, in white with green facings for the 1st Regiment and in white with red facings for the 2nd Regiment. This dress was retained in use until 1812.

Chasseurs de Montagne: Following his invasion of Spain, Napoleon decided in August 1808 to raise several special battalions of light infantry from the French departments bordering with Spain along the Pyrenees. The French Army had included special corps of light skirmishers from the mountains located on the frontier with Spain for many years. These were made up of *miquelets*, i.e. mountaineers who were used to living in the Pyrenees and who fought by using hit-and-run tactics. Now that the French Army's lines of communication and supply crossed the Pyrenees, Napoleon decided to revive the traditions of the *miquelets* by organizing units of mountain infantry that could patrol the frontier between France and Spain across the Pyrenees. The main task of the new Chasseurs de Montagne were to protect the lines of communication and supply of the French Army from attacks by Spanish insurgents, the *guerrilleros*, who organized effective ambushes and were superb skirmishers. The new battalions of mountain infantry, five in total, were recruited from the many young men of the Pyrenean departments who opposed conscription because they did not wish to leave their home territory in order to serve in the French Army. These individuals had frequently formed bands of brigands and survived by pillaging in the countryside, but now they had the opportunity to serve in the army but remain in their homeland. In exchange for pardon from the government, many volunteers enlisted in the new battalions, which had a variable number of companies: the Battalion of the Eastern

Grenadier of the Italian Legion.　Carabinier of the Tirailleurs du Po.

Uniforms of the Piedmontese Legion (from left to right): fusilier, grenadier and voltigeur.

Pyrenees, Battalion of the Upper Pyrenees, Battalion of the Lower Pyrenees and Battalion of Ariège each had eight companies, but the Battalion of Upper Garonne had only two companies. In the Lower Pyrenees and in Ariège, the local prefects had so many volunteers for the Chasseurs de Montagne that second battalions with eight companies apiece could be formed. Each mountain infantry company consisted of one captain, one lieutenant, one sub-lieutenant, one sergeant-major, four sergeants, one corporal-fourrier, eight corporals, one drummer and 130 privates.

Soon after their formation, however, the battalions of Chasseurs de Montagne were sent to fight in Spain as normal light infantry, and thus had to leave their home departments. This was felt to be a major betrayal by most of the *miquelets*, and thus many of them deserted soon after having been sent south of the mountains. On 17 January 1811, Napoleon was forced to reorganize his mountain infantry on just three battalions: the 1st Battalion comprised six companies from the Eastern Pyrenees, Upper-Garonne and the Upper-Pyrenees; the 2nd Battalion comprised eight companies from Ariège; and the 3rd Battalion comprised eight companies from the Lower Pyrenees. The Chasseurs de Montagne fought extremely well in Spain, where they were among the few French units that were able to counter the *guerrilleros* by using their same tactics. Following the French evacuation of Spain in 1814, the three battalions of mountain infantry were absorbed into other units: the 1st Battalion in the 116th Line Regiment, the 2nd Battalion in the 4th Light Regiment and the 3rd Battalion in the 25th Light Regiment. The Chasseurs de Montagne were dressed like the light infantry, but their uniform was entirely brown instead of medium blue, with light blue facings and piping.

Tirailleurs Corses: Corsica, the home of Napoleon, was annexed by France only in 1770, after having been under the control of Genoa for several centuries. During the French Revolution, the island revolted against the new republican government and was independent for a short period thanks to the military support provided by Britain. By 1797, however, the French had been able to reoccupy Corsica. On 8 July 1802, Napoleon decided to raise a light infantry battalion from the inhabitants of the island, who were raised as excellent hunters from their childhood and were used to living and moving on the mountainous terrain of their homeland. Initially, the light battalion recruited in Corsica was a normal unit of chasseurs; it became the 3rd Battalion of the 8th Light Infantry Regiment, but was quite autonomous from an administrative point of view. The unit consisted of nine active companies plus one depot company. In May 1804, the battalion was detached from its parent regiment and became a fully independent corps, assuming the new denomination of Tirailleurs Corses. Between 1805 and 1809, the Corsican light infantrymen participated in all the most important campaigns fought by the French Army, distinguishing themselves on several occasions. Their battalion now had a standard establishment with six companies. On 8 September 1811, the Tirailleurs Corses were disbanded and absorbed into the re-raised 11th Light Regiment (of which they became the 1st Battalion). In 1814, following Napoleon's first abdication, the restored monarchy decided to raise two new battalions of Tirailleurs Corses. When the emperor returned in 1815, he transferred these two units to mainland France in order to fight against the Allies, and organized another two battalions that would remain in Corsica. After the second abdication of Napoleon, all four battalions of Tirailleurs Corses were disbanded.

Until 1804, the Corsican light infantrymen were dressed exactly like the normal chasseurs, but with facings and piping of their medium blue uniform in green, and cords and flounders of their shako in green. In 1804, they received a distinctive uniform, which had the same cut and main features as that worn by the regular light infantrymen but was entirely brown. Facings and piping remained green on this new uniform, like the cords and flounders of the shako. Around 1808, the dress of the Tirailleurs Corses was modified, with the cuffs becoming pointed and the frontal lapels forming a single plastron like in the coats introduced by the Bardin Regulations. Collar, cuffs and frontal plastron became all red. The re-formed Tirailleurs Corses of 1815 received a new uniform that had as headgear a black Corsican hat with the left brim turned up, with a national cockade and pompom in company colour. The coat, always brown, was of the new model introduced in 1812 for all the French foot troops, and had collar, pointed cuffs and piping in green. Trousers, which had been brown until 1811, were now green. The personal equipment used by the Tirailleurs Corses was the same as that of the light infantry chasseurs, but included a peculiar ammunition pouch (*carchera*) that was carried on the stomach. All the belt equipment, including a single crossbelt for the bayonet and short sword, was in buff leather.

In addition to the Tirailleurs Corses, from 1803–05 the French Army also had five battalions of Corsican light infantry that were stationed on their home island in order to act against the local bands of bandits and insurgents who still resented French rule. Each of these territorial battalions of light infantry comprised one company of carabiniers and four companies of chasseurs. In 1806, since the island had been fully pacified, Napoleon decided to transfer the five units from Corsica to Italy, where the French Army was conquering the Kingdom of Naples. Before leaving Corsica, the five battalions of light infantry were assembled into a single corps known as the Corsican Legion. Once in Italy, all the carabinier companies of the new unit were amalgamated to form an elite carabinier battalion. After the French completed their conquest of

Grenadier
(left) and
voltigeur
(right) of the
Piedmontese
Legion.

the Kingdom of Naples, the Corsican Legion was transferred to the new Neapolitan Army that served Joseph Bonaparte, the new King of Naples. In November 1806, the Corsican Legion received the new denomination of Corsican Light Regiment and was reorganized on three battalions with nine companies each (one of carabiniers and eight of chasseurs). It remained part of the Neapolitan Army until 1813. The light infantrymen of the Corsican Legion were dressed exactly like the French chasseurs, but the collar of their coat was green.

Chasseur of the Hanoverian Legion.

Chapter 7

Foreign Infantry Units

Since the days of Louis XIV, in the last quarter of the seventeenth century, the French infantry had always included a sizeable number of foreign regiments. Some of these, such as the Swiss regiments, had an excellent military reputation and had been in the service of France since the late fifteenth century. During the French Revolution, many foreign volunteers went to France in order to fight under the flags of the new Republic, soon becoming an important component of the French military. Napoleon, after becoming First Consul in 1799, continued the traditional French policy of having substantial numbers of foreigners in the armed forces and sponsored the formation of several new corps made up of non-French soldiers.

Swiss Regiments: For several years after the fall of the monarchy in 1792, France did not have any Swiss infantry regiment, as all foreign military units had been disbanded. The Swiss soldiers had been the last defenders of the French royal family, and thus were particularly hated by the population who had rebelled against the Bourbon regime. In 1798, France invaded Switzerland as part of its revolutionary expansion, and the country was transformed into a puppet state known as the Helvetian Republic. After having obtained control over Switzerland, the French government asked the political representatives of the Helvetian Republic to raise a total of six line demi-brigades that would serve with the French Army. During 1799, however, Switzerland was also invaded by the Allies and became – for several months – the battlefield of the ongoing military confrontation between France and the Austro-Russians. In the early months of 1800, after the Helvetian Republic was brought back under French control, Napoleon could finally start his reorganization of the Swiss military forces. The First Consul was never particularly loved by the Swiss, since he wanted to transform the Helvetian Republic into a centralized state by abolishing the traditional administrative organization based on cantons. The Swiss were jealous of their cantonal autonomy, and thus vehemently opposed Napoleon's proposed reforms. The First Consul also aimed to create an autonomous Swiss Army that would be under the control of the Helvetian Republic (known as the Helvetian Legion), as well as four Swiss half-brigades that would be part of the French Army. After lengthy discussions with the Swiss authorities, a compromise

Uniforms of the La Tour d'Auvergne Regiment (from left to right): horn player of the voltigeurs, carabinier and chasseur.

was accepted by Napoleon in 1802, under which the Helvetian Legion was disbanded and the old cantonal militias were reformed. At the same time, however, the Swiss agreed to provide 16,000 soldiers organized into four line infantry regiments to the French Army. The new regiments were recruited between 1805 and 1807. It should be noted, however, that from 1799–1805, three under-strength Swiss demi-brigades

Carabinier of the La Tour d'Auvergne
Regiment.

served with the French Army instead of the six that had been required by the French in 1798.

The four Swiss regiments raised from 1805–07 soon proved to be excellent units, becoming well known for their valour and participating in all the most important military campaigns fought by the French Army between 1808 and 1814. Each of the four regiments comprised four active battalions plus an independent company of artillery, while a single battalion consisted of one grenadier company, one voltigeur company and seven fusilier companies. The regimental staff and the single companies had the same internal organization as the standard French companies. The artillery company, meanwhile, had four officers and sixty-four gunners who served two 4-pdr guns. In March 1812, after several years of service in Spain and after the Swiss Confederation signed a new capitulation with France, the four infantry regiments were reorganized. Each of them was now to have three active battalions instead of four, plus one depot half-battalion. The single artillery company in each regiment was retained, but was re-equipped with two 3-pdr guns. The new active battalions were smaller than the previous ones, since each of them was to comprise one grenadier company, one voltigeur company and just four fusilier companies. After the disastrous Russian campaign of 1812, which saw the participation of all the Swiss regiments, they were reorganized in 1813 as single-battalion regiments due to the heavy losses suffered. Following the restoration of the French royal family in 1814, what remained of the four Swiss regiments returned home. Although Napoleon tried to organize a new Swiss infantry regiment in 1815, structured on two battalions with Swiss soldiers who were still loyal to him, in the end only one battalion took part in the Belgian campaign that culminated with the Battle of Waterloo.

The three Swiss half-brigades of 1799–1805 were dressed in red, which was the traditional colour of the Swiss regiments in French service. Their uniforms were exactly the same as the French line infantry, but in red and with distinctive colours for facings and piping. The 1st demi-brigade had white facings and dark blue piping, the 2nd demi-brigade had dark blue facings and white piping, and the 3rd demi-brigade had yellow facings and sky blue piping. The trousers and waistcoats were dark blue until 1800, when they were replaced with white ones. The new four regiments organized between 1805 and 1807 continued to be dressed like the French line infantry, but again in red. The 1st Regiment had yellow facings and dark blue piping, the 2nd Regiment had dark blue facings and yellow piping, the 3rd Regiment had black facings and white piping, and the 4th Regiment had sky blue facings and white piping. The grenadiers of the Swiss regiments wore a peculiar bearskin having a brass frontal plate that bore an Imperial Eagle. The musicians wore uniforms in the piping colour of their regiment instead of red. In 1812, with the introduction of the Bardin Regulations, the colours of facings and piping were modified as follows: the 1st Regiment had yellow facings and yellow piping; the 2nd Regiment had dark blue facings and red piping; the 3rd Regiment had black facings and red piping; and the 4th Regiment had sky blue facings and red piping. In addition to the four Swiss regiments organized between 1805 and 1807, the French Army also included two independent battalions of Swiss infantry that were provided by two semi-autonomous areas of Switzerland: the Canton of Valais and the Principality of Neuchatel (neither of which were part of the Swiss Confederation, and thus are covered in separate sections below).

Valais Battalion: The Canton of Valais, located in south-west Switzerland, included the strategically important Alpine passes of Simplon and Great Saint Bernard. For this reason, Napoleon supported those political exponents of the canton who wanted to secede from the Swiss Confederation. In 1802, the Canton of Valais finally became independent under the protection of France. Consequently, in October 1805, Valais agreed to recruit a battalion of line infantry to serve with the French Army. The new unit had a small establishment, with just one grenadier company and four fusilier companies. Like all the other Swiss cantons, in addition to this battalion recruited for French service, Valais had an autonomous home-defence militia. Like the four Swiss regiments, the Valais Battalion was sent to Spain, where it fought with great distinction and suffered heavy losses. On 12 November 1810, Napoleon annexed the Canton of Valais to France, then in 1811 the Valais Battalion was incorporated into the new 11th Light Infantry of the French Army. The soldiers of the Valais Battalion were dressed like the French line infantry, but with red coats that had white facings and red piping. The grenadier company of the unit did not have bearskins, but wore shakos with red company distinctions.

Neuchatel Battalion: In 1806, the small Principality of Neuchatel, located in north-west Switzerland, was ceded to France by Prussia. Napoleon, instead of annexing the state to France, decided to give it to his loyal Chief-of-Staff, Marshal Berthier (who thereby became the Prince of Neuchatel). On 11 May 1807, the military forces of the Principality of Neuchatel were organized as a single line infantry battalion with six companies: one of grenadiers, one of voltigeurs and four of fusiliers (each with 160 men). Also attached to the battalion was a mixed company of artillery and engineers, consisting of four officers, fourteen NCOs, thirty-two gunners, sixteen wagon train drivers and sixteen sappers. The company was equipped with two 6-pdr guns. The Neuchatel Battalion served with distinction on several occasions, especially in Spain, until being officially disbanded in June 1814. The soldiers of the Neuchatel Battalion

Chasseurs of the Isembourg Regiment.

were known as 'canaries' because of their yellow uniforms; they were dressed like the French line infantry but with yellow coats that had red facings.

Italian Legion: In the spring of 1799, the Cisalpine Republic – the large puppet state of France, which had been created by Napoleon in northern Italy in 1797 – was invaded by an Austro-Russian force. The Cisalpine Army, which was quite large, was disbanded following the fall of the republic, but many of its members followed the French during their retreat as they wanted to continue serving under Napoleon.

As a result, the First Consul decided to create an Italian Legion within the French Army, made up of former Cisalpine soldiers. The new unit, formed on 8 September 1799, comprised four battalions of line infantry and four squadrons of mounted chasseurs, as well as one company of light artillery. Each of the infantry battalions had one company of grenadiers, one company of chasseurs and eight companies of fusiliers. In January 1800, another two battalions were added to the existing ones, but the Italian Legion was disbanded a few weeks later when the Cisalpine Republic was restored by the French following the Battle of Marengo. The infantry of the Italian Legion was dressed like the contemporary French light infantry, but in medium green instead of medium blue, and with yellow facings and piping. In addition to the Italian Legion, the French Army of 1799–1800 included an independent Italian Battalion of line infantry that was made up of political refugees from Italy. This was dressed like the French line infantry, but with collar and cuffs of the coat in green.

Tirailleurs du Po: In March 1801, the Duchy of Parma, one of the many small states of the Italian peninsula, was annexed by France and the army of the princedom was disbanded. In April 1803, Napoleon decided to raise a light infantry unit from the new Italian departments of France that had been organized on the territories of the former Duchy of Parma. This new corps, a battalion, assumed the denomination of the Tirailleurs du Po since most of its members came from the areas located on the banks of the Po River. The battalion consisted of one carabinier company and five

Chasseur of the Isembourg Regiment.

chasseur companies, and from 1805 onwards it served with distinction as part of the French Army, fighting at Austerlitz, Jena, Eylau and Friedland. The Italian soldiers of the Tirailleurs du Po were considered to be among the best light infantrymen in the French Army, and were particularly loved by Napoleon. In 1811, the battalion ceased to be an independent unit when it was absorbed into the new 11th Light Regiment of the French Army (becoming the 2nd Battalion of the regiment). The Tirailleurs du Po were dressed like the contemporary French light infantry, but retained the bicorn (with falling plume) as their headgear until 1811. In addition, their coats had collar, pointed cuffs, frontal lapels and turnbacks in red with white piping.

Piedmontese Legion: In 1799, what remained of the Piedmontese Army was absorbed into the French Army, since Piedmont (officially known as the Kingdom of Sardinia) was annexed to France. The Piedmontese soldiers were reorganized into two demi-brigades of line infantry, one demi-brigade of light infantry, one regiment of dragoons and one regiment of mounted chasseurs, but these units were soon disbanded and none of them were still in existence by 1803. The Piedmontese Army of pre-1799 also included five line infantry regiments of Swiss mercenaries; the French tried to retain in service these experienced soldiers by reorganizing them in two legions, but these too were very short-lived. Consequently, on 18 May 1803, Napoleon ordered the formation of four legions made up of former Piedmontese soldiers who were to be recruited from the Italian departments of the French Republic. Each legion was to comprise three battalions of line infantry, two battalions of light infantry and one company of artillery. Individual battalions would have consisted of one elite company of grenadiers or carabiniers and four companies of fusiliers and chasseurs. In the end, however, only one of the four planned legions could be formed; this became known as the Piedmontese Legion or the Légion du Midi. This unit served in Haiti before being reduced, in 1808, to just a single battalion of light infantry (with one company of carabiniers, one company of voltigeurs and three companies of chasseurs). The unit was then sent to Spain. Meanwhile, Napoleon organized a new Piedmontese battalion that became known as the 2nd Piedmontese Legion, but this was also very short-lived. In 1811, the 1st Piedmontese Legion was disbanded too. During its existence, members of the Piedmontese Legion wore two different uniforms. The first uniform, worn for just a few months during 1803, was like that of the French line infantry, but in grey with red facings/piping and the light infantry shako as headgear. The grey was soon replaced with dark brown, and the fusilier companies replaced their shako with a very peculiar helmet (similar to that worn by the French dragoons): this was made of black leather, with brass frontal plate and brass crest, and had a tufted pompom on the front of the crest in company colour. The facings and piping of the new uniform were light blue. The black helmet was retained in use until 1808, when it was replaced by the standard line infantry shako.

Hanoverian Legion: In 1803, following the French occupation of Hanover, which was a German state governed by the same royal family that ruled Great Britain, Napoleon decided to establish a legion made up of former members of the recently disbanded Hanoverian Army who wanted to serve under him. This new Hanoverian Legion was to consist of one light infantry regiment (with two battalions) and one regiment of mounted chasseurs (with four squadrons). However, desertion and sickness prevented the new corps from reaching its planned establishments. The unit served in Spain during the following years, where it performed auxiliary functions. On 10 March 1810, the Westphalian Battalion (another foreign unit that will be covered below) was absorbed into the Hanoverian Legion, which could thus finally reach its establishment of two battalions. On 11 August 1811, however, the corps was finally disbanded after having suffered severe losses in Spain. The infantry of the Hanoverian Legion was dressed like the French line infantry, but with red coats that had dark blue facings and piping. The coats for the new corps were initially produced from the stores of cloth found in the magazines of the Hanoverian Army (which was dressed in red like the British Army).

La Tour d'Auvergne Regiment: This unit was created in September 1805 and was made up of PoWs captured during the campaign fought against the Austro-Russians in 1805. The name of the corps, which was mostly composed of German-speaking soldiers, derived from its commander, the Prince of La Tour d'Auvergne. It consisted of three light infantry battalions with six companies each (one of carabiniers, one of voltigeurs and four of chasseurs). In 1809, with new Austrian PoWs captured at Wagram, a fourth battalion was added to the regiment. Two years later, in 1811, another two battalions made up of Spanish and Portuguese PoWs were added to the unit. In that same year, the corps assumed the new denomination of the 1st Foreign Regiment, but after being reduced to just four battalions, it was disbanded in the closing weeks of 1813. The soldiers of the La Tour d'Auvergne Regiment were dressed like the French light infantrymen, but entirely in dark green instead of medium blue, while the collar and cuff flaps of their coats were red.

Isembourg Regiment: This unit was created in November 1805 from PoWs captured during the campaign fought against the Austro-Russians in 1805. The name of the corps, which was mostly made up of German-speaking soldiers, derived from its commander, the Prince of Isembourg. It consisted of four light infantry battalions

Uniforms of the Prussian Regiment (from left to right): musicians, officer and privates.

with nine companies each (one of carabiniers, one of voltigeurs and seven of chasseurs). The Isembourg Regiment became in essence a 'foreign legion', because from 1809 it started to comprise an increasing number of Spanish and Portuguese PoWs. On 16 October 1810, the unit was reorganized on six battalions with six companies apiece, then on 3 August 1811 it was renamed the 2nd Foreign Regiment of the French Army. A few days after receiving the new denomination, the Isembourg Regiment

Soldiers of the Westphalia Regiment (left) and the Prussian Regiment (right).

absorbed what remained of the disbanded Hanoverian Legion. The corps ceased to exist in 1814, like most of the other foreign units of the French Army. The soldiers of the Isembourg Regiment were dressed like the French light infantrymen, but with collar and cuff flaps of their coats in yellow.

Prussian Regiment: Following the defeat of Prussia at Jena and Auerstadt, Naploeon decided on 13 November 1806 to raise a new infantry regiment from the many Prussian PoWs who were in French hands. The new unit, simply known as the Prussian Regiment, was structured on three battalions; the first of these served in Spain, while the other two fought against the British in the Netherlands in 1809. The Prussian Regiment always suffered from high desertion rates, and thus was never an elite unit. The number of its battalions was reduced from three to two in 1810, and the following year the unit became the new 4th Foreign Regiment of the French Army. After having been sent again to Spain and performed quite badly there, the Prussian Regiment was deployed as a garrison unit in the Netherlands before rebelling against the French authorities on 19 November 1813. A few days later, it was officially disbanded. The Prussian Regiment was uniformed like the French light infantry from its formation, but its coat and trousers were dark green, the former having red facings and piping. It should be noted, however, that the frontal lapels of the coat formed a single plastron before the introduction of this item in the 1812 dress regulations.

Westphalia Regiment: On 11 December 1806, Napoleon decreed the formation of a new foreign regiment made up of Prussian PoWs captured during the 1806 campaign. It consisted of four line infantry battalions with six companies apiece (one of grenadiers, one of voltigeurs and four of fusiliers). By June 1807, however, most of the unit's original soldiers had already deserted, so the regiment was restructured on just two battalions. In November 1807, the 1st Battalion was sent to Spain, where it was later absorbed into the Hanoverian Legion. The remaining 2nd Battalion then started to be known as the Westphalia Battalion. This continued to exist until 1813, when its members were absorbed into the army of the Kingdom of Westphalia (a puppet state of France). The soldiers of the Westphalia Regiment were dressed like the French line infantrymen, but their coats were white with red facings and piping.

Irish Legion: Following the Irish Rebellion of 1798, a number of Irish insurgents fled to France as political exiles. They soon formed quite a large community, and Napoleon saw that they could be organized into a military corps; the French Army, after all, had for several decades included several excellent Irish infantry units. On 31 August 1803, as part of Napoleon's planned invasion of Great Britain, a new Irish Legion was raised from the Irish refugees in France. The French had already organized a small Irish Legion in 1798 and had sent it to Ireland, together with other military units, in the hope of supporting the local insurgents who were rebelling against the British government. Members of this first legion, however, were very few in number, and the unit was extremely short-lived. The new Irish Legion created by Napoleon had a much longer existence. It initially consisted of only a single battalion, but was later expanded to become a regiment. The Irish soldiers, who were the only foreigners of the French Army to receive an Imperial Eagle as their standard, were mostly stationed along the coast of northern France to perform garrison duties. From 1808, however, two battalions of the legion were sent to Spain, where they distinguished themselves in action on several occasions. In October 1810, the two battalions fighting in Spain were brought together to form a single unit, which returned to France in 1811, when the whole Irish Legion received the new denomination of the 3rd Foreign Regiment. Napoleon had decided to reorganize some of his most important foreign units as four foreign regiments, numbered from the 1st to the 4th. During 1813 and 1814, the 3rd Foreign Regiment fought with great distinction in Germany, suffering heavy casualties, but following the first restoration of the French royal family, the two battalions of the unit were disbanded on 28 September 1814. The soldiers of the Irish Legion were always dressed like the French line infantrymen, but their coats were green (the Irish national colour) with yellow facings and piping.

Portuguese Legion: In 1807, the French Army occupied Portugal when its government refused to close ports to British military forces and merchant ships. After the Portuguese Army was disbanded, Napoleon decided to reorganize it as a 9,000-strong Portuguese Legion and make it part of the French Army. The new corps was established on 12 November 1807 and initially comprised the following units: five regiments of line infantry, one battalion of light infantry, three regiments of mounted chasseurs, one battery of artillery, one depot battalion of infantry and one depot squadron of cavalry. Very soon after its formation, however, many Portuguese soldiers deserted during their journey from Spain to France, and thus the Portuguese Legion was reduced to three regiments of line infantry, one regiment of mounted chasseurs and one depot battalion of infantry. The corps served with distinction in the Austrian campaign of 1809, and later took part in the disastrous Russian campaign of 1812. The Portuguese soldiers fought with great determination in Russia and were much admired by Napoleon. In 1813, after returning to France, the Portuguese Legion was reduced to just two battalions of infantry (one active and one depot), but it was disbanded on 5 May 1814 following the first abdication of Napoleon. The infantrymen of the Portuguese Legion were dressed in a distinctive brown uniform that was very dark in appearance, earning them the nickname of the Black Infantry. Their dress comprised the following elements: black shako with a crown that sloped down at the back in order to produce a false front, brass chinscales, brass frontal plate bearing unit number, black visor, brass unit badge (worn only by elite companies, with a flaming grenade for grenadiers and a hunting horn for chasseurs), cords and flounders in company colour (worn only by elite companies, in red for grenadiers and in green for chasseurs), plume (red tipped in yellow for fusiliers, red for grenadiers and green for chasseurs); dark brown coat with collar, round cuffs and frontal plastron in red with white piping, white short turnbacks with red piping and dark brown shoulder straps piped in red for fusiliers (replaced by red epaulettes for grenadiers and by green epaulettes with red crescent for chasseurs); dark brown trousers with red side-stripe; white spats and black shoes. During the summer months, white trousers were worn; these were quite loose and were decorated with three red stripes on each side, as well as with red decorative knots on the front.

Joseph Napoleon's Regiment: Until 1807, Spain was a loyal ally of Napoleon and thus fought together with the French against the Allies. The Spanish monarchy even sent an expeditionary force, made up of the best units of the Spanish Army, to the Baltic region in order to support the French Army

Grenadier of the Irish Legion.

Grenadier of the Irish Legion.

that was operating there. This expeditionary force, known as the Division of the North, comprised four regiments of line infantry and two battalions of light infantry, among other units. When Napoleon invaded Spain and forced the ruling king, Ferdinand VII, to abdicate, most of the Spanish soldiers stationed in the Baltic refused to continue serving with the French. Napoleon had proclaimed his brother, Joseph Bonaparte, as King of Spain and was determined to annex the whole Iberian peninsula to the French Empire. Against all odds, the Division of the North was evacuated from the Baltic thanks to the decisive support of the Royal Navy, and was able to return to Spain in order to fight against the French invaders. It should be noted, however, that before the evacuation could be completed, two Spanish line infantry regiments were surrounded and disarmed by the French. During the autumn of 1808, Napoleon decided to raise a new military unit from the Spanish PoWs who had been captured in the Baltic, and as a result, on 13 February 1809, Joseph Napoleon's Regiment came into existence. It consisted of four active battalions and one depot battalion, each active battalion having four companies of fusiliers, one company of grenadiers and one company of voltigeurs. The new formation was never particularly loyal to the French, and thus it was never sent to Spain. Joseph Bonaparte had wanted to include it in his newly organized Spanish Army, but this proved impossible due to its untrustworthiness. The regiment did, however, participate in the Russian campaign of 1812 and the fighting in Germany in 1813, before being reduced to two battalions in mid-1813. On 25 November 1813, the unit was officially disbanded. The soldiers of Joseph Bonaparte's Regiment were dressed like the French line infantrymen, but with white coats that had green facings and piping.

Polish Legions: The Poles were among the most numerous and loyal foreign soldiers of France's armies during the whole Napoleonic Period. They fought under the flags of the French Republic and later of the French Empire because they had one great objective: freeing their homeland from the foreign troops that had occupied it. In 1795, the Commonwealth of Poland and Lithuania had disappeared from the maps of Europe when it was partitioned between three great powers: Austria, Prussia and Russia. These nations were hated by the Polish population, but were also at war with Revolutionary France, so Poland and France had several enemies in common. After a Polish national uprising was crushed in 1794, thousands of Polish patriots who had fought for the freedom of their country left their homeland as political refugees, settling in France. Here they were organized into a Polish Legion that was to fight alongside the French, but since the new constitution of the French Republic did not allow the presence of foreign units inside the French Army, it was transferred to the recently established Cisalpine Army of northern Italy. The Polish soldiers fought extremely well on several occasions and were admired by Napoleon. Indeed, due to their success and to the arrival of hundreds of new volunteers, a 2nd Polish Legion was organized (which was also part of the Cisalpine Army). The Poles suffered great losses in Italy during 1799, the Allies having organized an effective counter-offensive while Napoleon was in Egypt. The 2nd Polish Legion was completely destroyed in the fighting and ceased to exist, while the 1st Legion was greatly reduced in numbers. With the temporary fall of the Cisalpine Republic, after his return to France, Napoleon decreed that foreign troops could now serve as part of the French Army. Consequently, the survivors of the 1st Polish Legion were reorganized as part of the Italian Legion and a new Danube Legion was formed on the Rhine by recruiting new Polish volunteers (who were mostly PoWs from the Austrian Army).

The Danube Legion was the first Polish military unit of the French Army, consisting of four line infantry battalions, four squadrons of lancers and one company of mounted artillery. The corps served on the Rhine and later fought in Italy at the Battle of Marengo. In December 1801, the 1st Polish Legion and the Danube Legion were amalgamated and reorganized as three demi-brigades of infantry: the 1st, 2nd and 3rd Polish half-brigades. The first two brigades were made up of former members of the 1st Polish Legion, while the other comprised former members of the Danube Legion. The 2nd and 3rd Polish demi-brigades were sent to Haiti by Napoleon in 1802, where they were completely destroyed by the rebels and outbreaks of yellow fever. In 1805, the 1st Polish half-brigade was renamed the 1st Polish Legion and was assigned to the army of the Kingdom of Italy (the direct heir of the Cisalpine Republic). In 1806, the Polish Legion – now consisting of just one line infantry regiment and one lancer regiment – was transferred to the army of the Kingdom of Naples (which had been recently conquered by the French). After a few months in southern Italy, however, the corps was disbanded. In 1807, during the war against Russia, Napoleon decided to raise a new Polish Legion from the many Polish PoWs who had previously served in the Prussian Army. This unit was known as the Northern Legion and was planned to consist of two sub-legions, with four infantry battalions in each. However, only the first sub-legion ever came into existence. This served with distinction until 1808, when it was absorbed into the army of the newly constituted Grand Duchy of Warsaw. After great sacrifices, the Poles fighting for Napoleon during 1807 and 1808 finally achieved their main objective: the creation of a new and independent Polish state in their homeland.

Before the birth of the Grand Duchy of Warsaw, which was a protectorate of the French Empire, Napoleon decided to raise a new and larger Polish legion that would be part of the French Army. He assembled the former members of the Polish Legion that was no longer in Neapolitan service with new volunteers and – in February 1807

Fusilier (left) and mounted chasseur (right) of the Portuguese Legion. Note the peculiar white trousers of the infantryman.

Grenadier of the Joseph Napoleon's Regiment (left) and carabinier of the Septinsular Battalion (right).

– was able to organize a new Legion of the Vistula that comprised three regiments of line infantry and one regiment of lancers. After having been part of the army of the Kingdom of Westphalia for a short period of time, the Vistula Legion was finally included among the units of the French Army on 21 February 1808. Two of its infantry regiments and the lancer regiment took part in the invasion of Spain. However, the lancers were disbanded in 1811 and were absorbed into a newly established French cavalry regiment. During their years spent in Spain, the Polish soldiers distinguished themselves on several occasions. In 1809, after having defeated the Austrians at the Battle of Wagram, the emperor decreed the formation of a 2nd Vistula Legion to be recruited from Polish PoWs who had previously been part of the Austrian Army. This new unit, however, consisted of just two infantry battalions and was very short-lived, being disbanded in February 1810. Its members thereafter became the 4th Infantry Regiment of the 1st Vistula Legion. In 1812, in view of the forthcoming Russian campaign, the number of battalions in each infantry regiment of the Vistula Legion was increased from two to three; in addition, a small battery with two 3-pdr guns was attached to each infantry regiment. Of the 7,000 Polish soldiers who followed Napoleon into Russia at the beginning of the campaign, only some 1,500 returned. Due to these massive losses, the Vistula Legion was reorganized on 18 June 1813 as the Vistula Regiment (which had two battalions). With the restoration of the French royal family in 1814, the Vistula Regiment was disbanded.

The infantry of the Danube Legion was dressed exactly like the French line infantry, while the lancers and mounted artillery of the corps had Polish-style uniforms. The three Polish demi-brigades formed in 1801 wore a distinctive national uniform with *czapka* headgear and *kurtka* tunic; the former had a squared top, while the latter had the frontal lapels that formed a single plastron and very short turnbacks. The uniform was as follows: dark blue *czapka* with white edging to the outer seams, black bottom band and visor, national cockade, white metal badge (a Polish cross for fusiliers, a flaming grenade for grenadiers and a hunting horn for chasseurs), plume in company colour (white for fusiliers, red for grenadiers and green for chasseurs), and cords and flounders in company colour; dark blue *kurtka* with collar, round cuffs, frontal plastron and short turnbacks in regimental colour; dark blue trousers; and black leather half-boots with top piping and frontal tassel in company colour. Fusiliers had dark blue shoulder straps piped in regimental colour, while grenadiers had red epaulettes and chasseurs had green epaulettes. The regimental colour of the 1st Polish demi-brigade (which remained in Italy) was red, whereas that of the 2nd Polish demi-brigade was yellow and that of the 3rd Polish demi-brigade was red. The soldiers of the two latter units, after arriving in Haiti, replaced their *czapka* with a more practical round hat made of straw. It should be noted that the battalions of the Polish half-brigades included one company of fusiliers less than their French equivalents, but had one company of chasseurs each. The infantry of the Northern Legion was dressed similarly to the demi-brigades of the previous years: black *czapka* with white edging to the outer seams, black bottom band and visor, national cockade, brass frontal plate bearing an Imperial Eagle, pompom and plume in company colour (light blue for fusiliers, red for grenadiers and yellow for voltigeurs), and cords and flounders in company colour (white for fusiliers, red for grenadiers and yellow for voltigeurs); dark blue *kurtka* with round cuffs, cuff flaps, frontal plastron and short turnbacks in red, and dark blue collar piped in red; dark blue trousers with red side-stripe; and black gaiters. Fusiliers had light blue epaulettes, while grenadiers had them in red and voltigeurs in yellow. The infantry of the Vistula Legion was dressed as follows: black *czapka* with white edging to the outer seams, black bottom band and visor, national cockade, brass frontal plate bearing an Imperial Eagle, pompom in company colour (light blue for fusiliers, red for grenadiers and yellow for voltigeurs), and cords and flounders in company colour (white for fusiliers, red for grenadiers and yellow for voltigeurs); dark blue *kurtka* with collar, pointed cuffs, frontal plastron and short turnbacks in yellow; white trousers; and black gaiters. Fusiliers had white epaulettes, while grenadiers had red epaulettes and for voltigeurs they were yellow. The *czapka* was later replaced by an ordinary shako, like that worn by the French line infantry.

Balkan Troops: During the Napoleonic Period, the French occupied – albeit for short periods – several areas of the Balkans and recruited a number of military units from them. The French controlled the following territories in the Balkans during the period 1797–1815: the Ionian Islands (also known as the Seven Islands, firstly from 1797–99, and then between 1807 and 1814), Dalmatia and Istria (which were annexed to the Kingdom of Italy from 1805–09 and then to the French Empire from 1809–14) and the Illyrian Provinces (which were part of the French Empire between 1809 and 1814). The Ionian Islands were part of the Republic of Venice's territories before 1797, but when the Venetian state was ceded by Napoleon to Austria with the Treaty of Campoformio, the territory (which controlled the southern entrance to the Adriatic Sea) was annexed for a first time by France. Great Britain and Russia were also interested in the conquest of the Ionian Islands, and thus their possession was particularly contested during the Napoleonic Period until the French reoccupied them in 1807. Dalmatia and Istria were obtained by Napoleon in 1805 following the Austrian defeat at Austerlitz. They were part of the Kingdom of Italy (a semi-independent state ruled by Napoleon) until 1809, but were later annexed to the new Illyrian Provinces when they were created in 1809. Following the Austrian defeat of

Infantrymen of the Northern Legion (from left to right): grenadier, fusilier and voltigeur.

Fusilier of the Vistula Legion.

1809 at Wagram, the French obtained further territories along the Illyrian coast, meaning the Austrians lost practically all their access to the Adriatic Sea. With the incorporation of the new territories, Napoleon could form the new Illyrian Provinces, which also included the small Republic of Ragusa that had been occupied by the French in 1806. The new Balkan provinces of the French Empire were divided into six districts and had a very large population. They were invaded by the Austrians and seized from the French during the closing months of 1813, with the decisive support of the Royal Navy.

On 12 December 1807, after having reconquered the Ionian Islands, the French raised an Albanian Regiment from the large Albanian community living on the archipelago. Since many Albanians from the Balkan mainland had abandoned their homeland to resettle as farmers on the Ionian Islands, it was not difficult for the French to find enough recruits for the new unit. This consisted of three light infantry battalions with nine companies in each. On 10 March 1808, the French authorities recruited a new military corps in the Ionian Islands, this time from the Greek community that lived there; this was known as the Greek Foot Chasseurs and consisted of a single battalion with eight light infantry companies. In July 1809, the new unit was absorbed into the Albanian Regiment, which was restructured on six battalions of six companies apiece. On 6 November 1813, after the British captured some of the Ionian Islands, the Albanian

Regiment was reduced to just two battalions, which were officially disbanded in June 1814 following Napoleon's first abdication. The soldiers of both the Albanian Regiment and the Greek Foot Chasseurs never received regular uniforms, but were dressed in their national costume, which included a tunic with short skirt (*tunique fustanelle*) that was worn under a short scarlet vest with sleeves open to the elbow and a thick goatskin cloak. In addition to the corps described above, the French raised another military unit from the Ionian Islands: the Septinsular Battalion, a light infantry battalion comprising six companies. This unit was made up of soldiers who had previously formed the Venetian garrison of the Ionian Islands. It was expanded to nine companies in 1808, but after it performed quite badly against the British, the battalion was finally disbanded in 1812. The soldiers of the Septinsular Battalion were dressed exactly like the French light infantry, but with light blue facings and piping (including the side-stripe on the trousers).

During his Egyptian campaign of 1798–99, Napoleon recruited large numbers of foreigners (Greeks, Copts, Turks and Syrians) as auxiliaries. When the French left Egypt in 1801, several of these soldiers went to France, where they were reorganized as a light infantry battalion with eight companies (later increased to ten) that was known as the Oriental Chasseurs. This unit served with distinction and was later attached to the Albanian Regiment of the Ionian Islands in 1809. The unit fought in several campaigns on mainland Europe until being disbanded on 24 September 1814. The Oriental Chasseurs were dressed like a normal light infantry battalion of the French Army.

After Napoleon annexed the whole of Illyria to his empire in 1809, the French inherited six regiments of Grenz (frontier) infantry from the Austrian Empire. In order to protect their Illyrian territories from incursions by the Ottomans, the Austrians had raised six regiments of light infantry from the warlike communities of the Balkan coastline. The frontier soldiers of Illyria lived in military settlements that were located along the border with the Ottoman Empire and were organized according to the *zadruga* system (which was based on extended family homesteads). Most of the frontier soldiers were Croats, but there were also significant numbers of Christian refugees from Bosnia. They were extremely loyal to the Austrian government, since it was from the latter that they received their farms in exchange for military service. the Grenzers were famous for their tactical skills as light infantry skirmishers, and were used to fighting on mountainous terrain. With the French occupation of Illyria, Napoleon came to have a total of 16,000 frontier soldiers under his command; these had been released from their oath of allegiance to the Austrian Empire and could now serve as part of the French Army. They were reorganized as six regiments of Illyrian Chasseurs, which were also known as Croatian Regiments.

The original Austrian internal composition of the units was retained, and thus each regiment comprised two active battalions (with six light companies each), plus a depot with two companies. In case of war, the number of active battalions was increased to four, the two depot companies being enlarged to become battalions. In 1812, the internal establishment of the regiments of Illyrian Chasseurs was increased from two to three active battalions. During the following year, however, the Austrians invaded Illyria and the great majority of the former Grenzers abandoned the French to re-enter the ranks of the Austrian Army. Until 22 May 1810, the Illyrian Chasseurs continued to wear their old Austrian uniforms, but thereafter a new dress in the French style was introduced. This comprised a standard black shako and a medium blue single-breasted coat with collar, pointed cuffs, frontal piping and turnbacks in regimental colour. The uniform was completed by a white waistcoat, medium blue trousers and black half-boots. Regimental colours were as follows: red for the 1st Regiment, crimson for the 2nd Regiment, yellow for the 3rd Regiment, violet for the 4th Regiment, sky blue for the 5th Regiment and green for the 6th Regiment.

In order to have some battalions of Illyrian Chasseurs available for military service outside their home territories, in 1811 Napoleon ordered the formation of several Croatian Provisional Regiments to be created by assembling together the active battalions provided for external service by each regiment of Illyrian Chasseurs. Since each regiment provided one or two battalions for external service, it was possible to create four Croatian Provisional Regiments with two battalions each. These battalions had the same internal structure as the French light infantry battalions, with one company of carabiniers, one company of voltigeurs and four companies of chasseurs. The first three Croatian Provisional Regiments fought with great determination as part of the French Army in the campaigns of 1812 and 1813, whereas the fourth was mostly deployed in Italy and saw no combat. All four regiments were disbanded in January 1814, mostly due to the heavy losses they had suffered. In January 1812, to be easily distinguishable from their parent units of the Illyrian Chasseurs, the Croatian Provisional Regiments received a distinctive uniform like that worn by the French light infantry regiments, but entirely in medium green (instead of medium blue) and with yellow facings and piping. The trousers they wore were quite peculiar, since they had yellow side-stripes and yellow decorative knots on the front. In the early months of 1810, Napoleon decided to raise another regular military unit from his Illyrian Provinces, to be made up of soldiers from the non-frontier areas of Illyria. The new corps was known as the Illyrian Regiment and was structured on five battalions of light infantry (four active and one in the depot). The unit served with distinction in Russia, where it suffered severe losses, and was disbanded on 17 November 1813. The Illyrian

Officer of the 6th Regiment of
Illyrian Chasseurs.

Soldier of the 1st Regiment of
Illyrian Chasseurs.

Regiment was dressed exactly like the French light infantry, but with red collar and pointed cuffs piped in white, while its members also had red shoulder wings piped in white on their coats.

In addition to the regular units described above, the French also recruited sizeable numbers of irregulars from the Illyrian Provinces, namely the Serezaners and the Pandours. The Serezaners were first raised by the Austrian authorities in the 1790s from Bosnian refugees who had settled on Croatian lands, and were organized into companies of 200 men each, which were attached to the regiments of Grenzers. Each regiment of frontier infantry had its own company of Serezaners, who acted as scouts during times of war and as frontier guards in peacetime. These irregulars did not have uniforms, instead wearing their national dress that comprised the following elements: red pointed hat during winter or red cap in the summer, white or blue loose shirt, red or blue waistcoat decorated with silver rings and buttons, loose coloured trousers and soft leather shoes. Like the Pandours and the semi-regular units recruited in the Ionian Islands, the Serezaners were armed with a bewildering variety of locally manufactured traditional weapons, including long-barrelled muskets, pistols, curved sabres and knives.

The Pandours made up an irregular corps of militarized policemen who had been tasked (since 1748) with guarding the Balkan frontier of the Austrian Empire in Bosnia against the incursions of the Ottomans. On 17 March 1810, they were reorganized by the French as part of the military forces of the Illyrian Provinces and received the new name of the Corps of Dalmatian Pandours. In exchange for their services, these irregulars were exempted from the usual labour obligations of the Balkan peasants. They trained every Sunday after the Mass and were recognized as excellent marksmen. The Corps of Dalmatian Pandours consisted of nine companies, which included the following officers and NCOs: one colonel, three battalion commanders, five adjutant-majors, nine captains, one paymaster, nine lieutenants, nine sub-lieutenants, twenty-seven sergeant-majors and fifty-four sergeants. Each company comprised one captain, one lieutenant, one sub-lieutenant, three sergeant-majors, six sergeants and either thirty-six or forty-eight rankers (including two drummers). When the Austrians invaded the Illyrian Provinces in 1813, the Pandours were the only Balkan soldiers to remain loyal to the French, but their corps was disbanded soon after the victory of the Austrians. On the day of their reorganization, in March 1810, the Pandours had received the following uniform: red turban, red waistcoat, red dolman jacket with silver lacing and lambswool trimming, blue trousers and brown sandals. This was later replaced by a new uniform that included a standard black shako, dark blue dolman jacket with red collar and round cuffs having white frontal frogging, dark blue trousers with white side-stripe and decorative knots on the front, and brown sandals. In addition to the Dalmatian Pandours, in June 1810, the French authorities also formed an independent Corps of Albanian Pandours that was tasked with protecting the southern Bay of Cattaro from incursions by Montenegrin raiders. This unit consisted of six companies (later increased to eight), but they were all disbanded by 1813. The Albanian Pandours wore the same uniform that was introduced in 1810 for the Dalmatian Pandours.

Soldier of the Croatian Provisional Regiments.

Bibliography

Brnardic, V., *Napoleon's Balkan Troops* (Osprey Publishing, 2004).

Bucquoy, E.L., *Gardes d'honneur et troupes étrangères* (Grancher, 1977–1985).

Bukhari, E., *French Napoleonic Line Infantry 1796–1815* (Almark Publishing, 1973).

Crowdy, T., *French Napoleonic Infantryman 1803–1815* (Osprey Publishing, 2002).

Crowdy, T., *French Revolutionary Infantry 1789–1802* (Osprey Publishing, 2004).

Crowdy, T., *French Revolutionary Infantryman 1793–1815* (Osprey Publishing, 2003).

Dempsey, G.C., *Napoleon's mercenaries: Foreign Units in the French Army under the Consulate and Empire 1799 to 1814* (Frontline Books, 2016).

Elting, J.R., *Napoleonic Uniforms* (Pearson, 1993–2000).

Elting, J.R., *Swords around a Throne: Napoleon's Grande Armée* (Free Press, 1988).

Fieffé, E., *Histoire des Troupes Etrangères au Service de France* (Librairie Militaire, 1854).

Funcken, F. & Funcken, L., *Les Soldats de la Revolution Française* (Casterman, 1988).

Greentree, D. & Campbell, D., *Napoleon's Swiss Troops* (Osprey Publishing, 2012).

Haythornthwaite, P., *Napoleon's Light Infantry* (Osprey Publishing, 1983).

Haythornthwaite, P., *Napoleon's Line Infantry* (Osprey Publishing, 1983).

Haythornthwaite, P., *Uniforms of the Peninsular War 1807–1814* (Blandford Press, 1978).

Haythornthwaite, P., *Uniforms of the Retreat from Moscow 1812* (Blandford Press, 1976).

Haythornthwaite, P., *Uniforms of Waterloo* (Blandford Press, 1986).

Jouineau, A. & Mongin, J.M., *French Line Infantry 1776–1810* (Editions Heimdal, 2021).

Jouineau, A. & Mongin, J.M., *French Line Infantry 1814–1845* (Editions Heimdal, 2021).

Jouineau, A. & Mongin, J.M., *The Swiss at the service of France 1715–1820* (Editions Heimdal, 2019).

Morawski, R. & Dusiewicz, A., *The Polish Army under Napoleon's command* (Karabela Publishing, 2010).

Index